SELF PUBLISHING TO AMAZON KDP IN 2023

A BEGINNERS GUIDE TO SELLING E-BOOKS, AUDIOBOOKS & PAPERBACKS ON AMAZON, AUDIBLE & BEYOND

BRIAN CHESSON

CONTENTS

INTRO

So, check this out: You might be sitting there, thinking, "Whoa, this book is on the shorter side!" But guess what? That's totally intentional. I didn't want to pad it with useless fluff and pointless rambling just to hit some arbitrary page count. Instead, I laser-focused on delivering the goods, taking you from point A to point B with maximum efficiency. Why waste your precious time sifting through hundreds of pages when I can give you all the knowledge you need in under two hours?

So, hold up before you judge this book solely based on its page count. Despite its brevity, let me assure you that every single word is packed with my years of hard-earned business wisdom. I'm all about providing you with valuable information that you can put into action right away.

Now, I can practically hear your brain buzzing with another question: "Why are you spilling all the secrets? What's in it for you?" Well, let me drop a truth bomb on you. Over the years, I've discovered that having an abundance mindset beats the pants off a scarcity mindset any day. When you truly believe there's an abundance of resources out there, you attract more of it into your life. It's like magic. So, I'm here to share the wealth and spread the knowledge far and wide.

Oh, and here's a little secret within the secret. While I'm sharing this book with the world, truth be told, it's really a love letter to my brother and cousin. This business model I'm about to unravel is pure gold. I've tried my hand at countless ventures, but I always find myself coming back to this gem. And now, I want to pass on all the wisdom I've gathered over the years and hand-deliver all the answers right to you. So buckle up, and embark on this thrilling journey with an open mind. Trust me, you're in for a wild ride filled with excitement at every turn!

Moving forward, please keep in mind two things: all prices quoted are in US dollars, and for your convenience, all the links featured in the book are conveniently compiled on a single page at the end, ensuring you won't have to search for them again.

1

THE BEGINNING

Picture this: It's 2019 and I'm broke as a joke after my epic year-long European adventure. I'm desperate for some cash and end up resorting to the ultimate money-making activity—watching YouTube videos. I stumbled upon this dude named Stephan James blabbering about something called Kindle Direct Publishing (KDP). Apparently, you can write books, toss 'em on Amazon, and voila, passive income in your pocket!

Intrigued, I went down the YouTube rabbit hole, binging on more videos than I'd care to admit. I mean, I was determined to debunk this whole thing as a scam. But guess what? Those sneaky YouTubers actually made sense! Their logic was solid and I couldn't argue with it. So, I thought, "Hey, why not? If it fails, I've only wasted a bit of my precious time."

According to Mr. James, the first step was to write about something you're ridiculously knowledgeable and passionate about—something you could ramble on about for hours without boring yourself to tears. Well, lucky for me, I had been deep into growing and selling Instagram accounts. It was still fresh in my brain, so I sat down and unleashed 10,000 words onto the digital canvas within a single week. Yeah, you heard me right. I was pretty much twiddling my thumbs all day, so 2,000 words a day was a piece of cake.

After conjuring up my masterpiece, aka *Instagram Mastery*, I took matters into my own hands. I whipped up a cover on Canva—a design platform that saved my artistic bacon—and formatted the whole thing using good ol' Google Docs. With trembling hands, I uploaded my precious files to KDP and eagerly waited for the magic to happen. Lo and behold, a day later my eBook and paperback were live on Amazon! And get this, I made my first-ever sale, raking in a whopping $2 in royalties! Two bucks, baby! I was on cloud nine, shouting from the rooftops, "It actually works! This ain't no scam!"

At that point, I was all in. I set a lofty goal for myself: to reach a monthly income of $2,000. Sure, it seemed like a daunting task. I mean, it would require me to repeat the process a thousand times. But hey, I've never been one to shy away from a challenge.

But here's the plot twist. I didn't need to churn out a thousand books to hit my goal. Heck, not even a hundred! Just a few months later, armed with a mere two dozen books, I was making a cool $2,000 per month! Talk about a pleasant surprise. Fast forward five years, and I'm still rocking the publishing game, pulling in over $10,000 each month. Can you believe it?

Now, let me drop some wisdom on you. You ready? Lean in. You don't need a mountain of books to hit that sweet $2,000/month mark. Nope, not even close, my fellow aspiring authors. It can be done with way less.

So, strap yourselves in, my curious comrades, because I'm about to spill the beans on how I'd conquer the publishing world if I were to embark on this wild ride all over again.

2

SELF PUBLISHING VS TRADITIONAL PUBLISHING

<u>Firstly, Why Self Publish?</u>

Do you know how to get a traditional publishing deal? Yeah, me neither. And from people I've heard who have, it's a huge process that leads to people hating their own book by the end of it. The money? A pittance. Authors usually receive a fraction of the sale of the book (around 10%). Plus they find out later that traditional publishing houses don't even promote their book. You need to go out and do that yourself.

On the other hand, Amazon gives you 60% of the royalty of the book (after the printing cost) and 70% of the sale of the eBook.

So, if the paperback was $14.99 you would receive approximately $6.

If your e-book was $2.99, you would receive approximately $2. (There is a small fee for large Kindle books to cover the digital files stored on Amazon's servers. This means that if your eBook file is quite large, especially with numerous images, it may result in a lower royalty).

So, although traditional publishers find a cover for your book and format it for you, it's not worth it. With self-publishing, you won't have any publishing deadlines either, which means no one is breathing down your neck and you can go at your own pace.

I'll teach you where and how to hire designers, formatters, and all that stuff in the following chapters.

Should I Only Publish On Amazon?

Yes. They are the biggest marketplace for books holding almost half of all print book sales and over seventy percent of eBook sales. They sell all over the world. Countries like Canada, UK, Australia, Japan, Germany, Italy and more! They're literally adding countries every other month (I recently saw that they added Poland). So being on Amazon gives you international buyers. And all you have to do is upload your book, they take care of the rest.

If that isn't enough, here's one more reason to only stick with Amazon.

There's this rule I learned over the last few years in business called Pareto's 80/20 rule. It states that approximately 80% of the results or outcomes come from 20% of the causes or efforts. The ratio might vary, perhaps being 90/10 or 70/30, but the underlying premise remains the same; a minority of inputs or activities frequently leads to the majority of the results or outputs.

In short, it means that you can make 80% of the money by doing 20% of the work. The 20% of the work is uploading your book to Amazon then moving onto the next one. Pursuing the remaining 20% revenue would require 80% more work, a disproportion that simply doesn't make sense. It's a principle that encourages efficiency, urging us to focus on what truly matters and not get lost in diminishing returns.

3

WHAT DO YOU PUBLISH?

There are four categories I think books can fall into. No content, low-content, fiction, and non-fiction books.

No Content

Also known as blank books or empty books, no content books are books that contain no predefined content or text. These books are intentionally left completely blank, without any lines, prompts, or illustrations. They provide empty pages or space for individuals to freely express their own ideas, thoughts, drawings, or whatever they desire. Examples include blank journals or notebooks.

Low Content

A type of book that typically contains minimal written words in it. These books often focus on providing space for users to engage in activities such as journaling, coloring, sketching, or keeping records. Examples of low-content books include notebooks, planners, coloring books, puzzle books, and diaries.

Fiction

Literary works that tell imaginative stories or narratives created by the author. They are not based on real events or people, but rather the product of the author's creativity and imagination. Fiction books encompass a wide range of genres, including romance, mystery, science fiction, fantasy, historical fiction, and more.

Non-Fiction

Literary works that provide factual information or present real events, ideas, and concepts. Unlike fiction books, non-fiction books are based on reality and aim to educate, inform, or explore various subjects. They cover a wide range of topics, including history, biographies, self-help, science, technology, philosophy, politics, and more.

So What Should I Publish?

I've tried them all, and if you're looking for my recommendation, I'd say go for non-fiction books. Making no content and low-content books is a breeze and super quick, making it easy to get started. But here's the catch: standing out is tough because of the fierce competition.

That's not to say it can't be done, but it's definitely harder. Plus, you have to price your book lower, around $6.99, to stay competitive. That means you only earn about $2 in royalties per book, leaving little room for ads (we'll talk about those later). On top of that, making money becomes tougher because you'd need to sell around fifty copies just to make $100. In comparison, it's actually easier to sell twenty copies of a different book that makes $5 each.

Oh, and there are big players in this space—companies and folks who have been around the block. They know the game inside out and can run circles around you. They play by different rules, like breaking even or even losing money on a book, all to hook readers and make more money from them in the future.

One more thing: low-content books won't work as e-books or audiobooks, so you're missing out on extra income streams.

When it comes to fiction books, it's important to have strong writing skills, which unfortunately, I lack. To tackle this, I hired ghostwriters to create some books for me, and they performed decently. However, relying on fiction ghostwriters means you're dependent on their availability. If they happen to leave, it can be quite a hassle to find another writer who can match their style.

Another aspect to keep in mind with fiction books is the reading preferences of the audience. Fiction readers tend to lean towards e-books rather than paperbacks, resulting in lower royalties (around $2 compared to $5 or more for paperbacks). Additionally, targeting specific keywords for marketing purposes can be challenging for fiction books (which we'll delve into in the next chapter).

By the way, non-fiction books encompass a wide range of genres, like cookbooks and travel books. However, I'd advise against venturing into those areas. They require colored images, which can be quite expensive to source, and the printing costs for colored images are higher than for black and white ones. This means overall expenses go up while royalties go down.

So, taking all of that into account, I hope you've come to the same conclusion as I have: non-fiction books (without colored images) are the way to go.

4

KEYWORDS

What's A Keyword?

Keywords hold a pivotal place in the world of book publishing, significantly influencing marketing strategies and discoverability. At their core, keywords are specific words or phrases that encapsulate the content of your book, facilitating readers in navigating the overwhelming ocean of book titles available. They act like signposts, steering potential readers towards books that resonate with their interests and tastes.

Put simply, or in a way I like to perceive it, a keyword is what someone would punch into the Amazon search bar on their home computer or mobile device. Imagine a friend, your parent, or grandparent hunting for a book on Amazon. Most likely, their search bar entry is your keyword. Here are some illustrations of what a keyword might be:

- Ketogenic diet for women
- Gardening in a small backyard
- Stretching techniques for seniors

- Puppy training methods
- Kid-friendly riddles

The common mistake many authors make is crafting a book and then wondering why it's not selling. One significant factor behind this is the absence of relevant keywords. Even the most excellent book will remain undiscovered if it can't be found. Hence, our approach should be different - we need to ensure people are actively searching for the keywords we're incorporating in our title even before we commence writing.

How To Find A Keyword?

When delving into the search for the right keywords, it's crucial to grasp several related terms that help us categorize and understand the subject matter more precisely.

At the broadest level, we encounter the concept of a "niche." Essentially, a niche is a category or area of interest containing various subtopics. It's a general umbrella under which more specific themes reside. The terms "niche" and "category" can be used interchangeably, with "pet training" serving as a typical example.

Within a niche, we find "subniches." These allow us to narrow our focus and zoom in on more specific areas of interest within the broader subject. If we consider "pet training" as a niche, then "cat training" would be an illustrative subniche.

Digging further, we reach the "book topic," the most specific level within a subniche. This is the heart of your content, the particular subject your book explores, and can be seen as a key keyword for your work. For instance, "Clicker Training for Cats" might be the book topic within the "cat training" subniche.

To provide a clearer understanding, let's break down a couple of examples:

For books related to animals:

• Broad category: books on animals

• Subcategory: books on pets

• Sub-subcategory: books on cats

• And so on, down to: books on clicker training for shy or fearful siamese cats

Similarly, in cooking:

• Broad category: cooking

• Subcategory: international cuisine

• Sub-subcategory: Italian cuisine

• And so on, down to: gluten-free hand-rolled gnocchi with vegan sauces

These examples illustrate how we can progressively narrow our focus from a broad category to a highly specific subject. Understanding these levels can guide you in targeting your intended audience effectively and selecting the most relevant keywords.

To find relevant keywords, we can begin by exploring Amazon's main niches. A simple way to access these niches is by searching for "Amazon book best sellers lists" on Google and clicking on the first link.

Once on the page, you will notice a list of categories on the left-hand side. These categories include a diverse range of topics, such as Arts & Photography, Business & Investing, Education & Reference, Health, Fitness & Dieting, Self-Help and more.

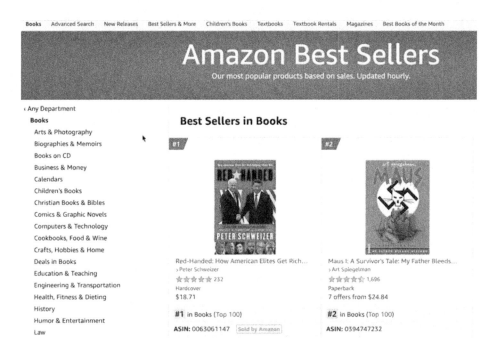

To narrow down our focus, we should avoid creating a book within a main niche as it tends to be too broad and highly competitive. Instead, let's click on a category within a niche, delving deeper into more specific layers. For example, in this case, we can choose to explore the "Crafts, Hobbies & Home" category. Within that category, we can go even deeper by clicking on "Crafts & Hobbies" and then narrowing down further to something like "Candlemaking."

So in summary we just clicked:

Crafts, Hobbies & Home —> Crafts & Hobbies —> Candlemaking

(Niche) —> (Sub-niche) —> (Keyword)

In exploring these subjects, you'll notice that we are delving into quite specialized topics, often outside the realm of conventional thought. You might find yourself wondering, "How large could the audience possibly be for books on something as specific as candle making?" Yet, it's often said that the riches are in the niches, and the audience for these specialized topics may be larger than you'd expect. By focusing on these unique niches, you're likely to encounter less competition, making them ideal targets for finding your keywords and creating your book.

Here are some examples of keywords I have found for you:

- Beekeeping for beginners
- Gut health
- Rental property investing
- Chess for kids
- Off-grid living
- Budgeting for college students
- Food truck business
- Meditation for entrepreneurs
- How to small talk
- Public speaking for beginners
- Leadership for women
- Cognitive behavioral therapy
- Social media marketing
- How to read music
- At-home workouts
- Decluttering your home

. . .

Some examples of how to go deeper into a niche is to add words like "for beginners/experts/seniors" or "for men/women."

Ketogenic diet —> "Ketogenic diet for beginners" or "Ketogenic diet for seniors" or even "Ketogenic diet for women over 50."

Let's explore what does not qualify as a keyword:

• Self-help

• Exercise

• Diet

• Music

• Outdoors

• Love

• Why anxiety sucks

• I can't lose weight

• Atomic habits

• Think and grow rich

• Money secrets

• Tony Robbins

• Money magic

• Weight loss magic for women

• Math

It's possible that some of these caught your attention as potential keywords. While they may hold relevance, they fall into the category of being too broad and lacking the necessary niche focus. You might have even recognized a few titles or names among them. However, it's crucial to be aware that incorporating famous names into your book title can result in complications with Amazon's guidelines.

Keyword Profitability

Now, let's delve into the profitability of our keywords. It's crucial to assess whether they have the potential to yield profitable results.

To determine this, we need to familiarize ourselves with the concept of BSR, which stands for Best Sellers Rank. This numerical value is updated on an hourly basis on Amazon and serves as an indicator of a book's sales performance.

In essence, a BSR of 1 signifies that the book holds the coveted title of being the number one best-selling book on Amazon. On the other hand, a BSR of 100,000 indicates that the book currently ranks as the 100,000th best-selling book on Amazon.

It's important to note that BSRs exist for each book format, including eBooks, paperbacks, and hardbacks. When assessing the profitability of a keyword, we consider BSR values of 100,000 or lower as highly desirable.

In summary, a lower BSR signifies higher sales volume and greater profitability. Therefore, when selecting keywords, it's advantageous to target those that have a BSR of 100,000 or less across the various book formats available on Amazon.

To see the BSR of a book, scroll down the book page on Amazon to the Product details to see all of its information:

Product details

ASIN : B0875Z2J69

Publisher : Independently published (April 14, 2020)

Language : English

Paperback : 132 pages

ISBN-13 : 979-8637201709

Item Weight : 7.8 ounces

Dimensions : 6 x 0.33 x 9 inches

Best Sellers Rank: #39,569 in Books (See Top 100 in Books)

   #1 in Candle Making (Books)

   #2 in Business of Art Reference

   #46 in Crafts & Hobbies Reference

Customer Reviews: 4.6 ⭐⭐⭐⭐✩ ⌄   697 ratings

Useful Tools

To be able to see BSR at a quick glance on the Amazon search page and not the book product page, I recommend downloading a free Chrome extension plugin called DS Amazon quick view. Simply Google it and click the first link.

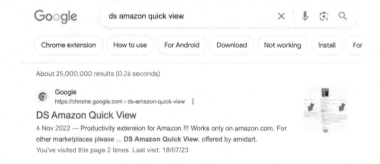

Now you should see the BSR number below each book on Amazon like this:

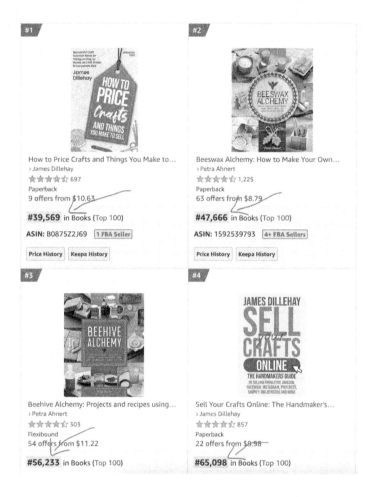

KDSpy

Another valuable tool that I highly recommend is KDSpy. It's not available for free unfortunately and is a one-time payment of $69. So, what exactly is KDSpy? It's a convenient Chrome extension that effortlessly extracts book data from the first page of search results and presents it in a well-organized manner.

Why is this tool so valuable? It provides a comprehensive overview of a book topic's competition and sales figures, granting you valuable insights. While it's possible to conduct research and assess profitability without this tool, it can be an incredibly time-consuming and challenging endeavor. Sometimes, in order to make money, we must be willing to invest some money, and KDSpy is an investment that will prove worthwhile.

By leveraging KDSpy, you gain a significant advantage, allowing you to streamline your research process and make informed decisions with greater ease. It simplifies the complexities of market analysis, empowering you to navigate the publishing landscape more effectively. There's a link at the back of the book to get it. These are the only two tools you'll need for keyword research.

Analyzing The Data

Let's look at how it works. We'll use "Candle making" as our keyword. Once we've typed that into Amazon, we're going to click the Chrome extension and KDSpy is going to do its thing. We now have all the information of the books on the first page.

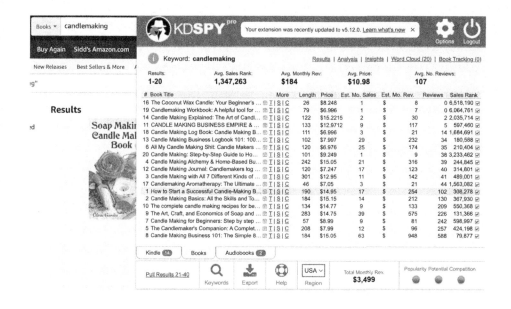

Let's focus our attention on two crucial columns: "Estimated monthly revenue (Est. Mo. Rev.)" and "reviews." It's important to clarify that the revenue figure displayed does not represent the author's profit. Instead, it reflects the earnings generated by Amazon. For instance, if we observe a highlighted revenue of $254, it means that Amazon is making that amount, while the author typically receives around one-third of that, approximately $84.

Moving on, our goal is to identify books with 100 reviews or less. Why this threshold? It's because if books with fewer than 100 reviews are generating profits, it indicates a higher likelihood that if we create our own book and gather a few reviews (fifteen to thirty is enough social proof), we too can potentially achieve a similar level of success.

By focusing on books that have garnered relatively fewer reviews, we open ourselves up to the possibility of tapping into a market where there is less competition. This paves the way for us to make a significant impact and potentially generate substantial earnings with our own book, especially if we can gather a few positive reviews to support its promotion and credibility.

What To Look For

Let's analyze the keyword example of Candlemaking. When we consider books with less than 100 reviews, the maximum revenue observed is $316, or a profit of $105. Ideally, I prefer to see at least two other books generating a similar level of revenue. This pattern strengthens my confidence that there is sufficient demand for this topic. If I were to write a book focusing on this keyword, it reassures me that there is a viable market and a greater chance of achieving the same financial success as those other titles.

Unfortunately, in this case, I don't see that demand for the keyword. However, I did come across one book with 34 reviews that earns $232, and another book with 102 reviews that brings in $254. Consequently, if we were to create an exceptional book on Candle making, the most we can expect to earn falls within this range (between $232 and $316 in revenue). While it's not an unfavorable outcome, considering the significant effort involved in producing the book, it may not be the most lucrative option. Therefore, it would be wise to explore alternative keywords.

As we continue our search, a favorable target to aim for is a keyword with three books under 100 reviews, each generating a minimum of $500 in monthly revenue. While two books may be acceptable, the more books that meet this criteria, the better. It serves as further evidence of the keyword's profitability, instilling greater confidence in our decision.

. . .

Conclusion

Ensuring that the keyword you entered is present in the book's title holds utmost importance. It safeguards against irrelevant search results that may appear, allowing you to maintain relevance and accuracy. To confirm this, a simple action of hovering over the book title and reading it in its entirety will suffice. When you spot the keyword within the title, consider it a positive sign indicating that you're on the right path towards achieving success.

Additionally, conducting your searches in an incognito window is highly recommended. This helps eliminate potential biases caused by data saved in your browser. By opting for this approach, you can access unbiased information, enabling you to make well-informed decisions based on accurate data.

In summary, the key question to ask yourself is: Are there a minimum of three books with under 100 reviews, each making at least $500 or more, and featuring the keyword in their book titles? If you come across a keyword that satisfies these conditions, you can confidently proceed. However, if not, unless it happens to be your first book, it's advisable not to proceed. Creating a book that lacks demand or market interest will only lead to wasted time and effort, without yielding the desired results of attracting readers and generating sales.

Chapter Summary

Understanding Keywords

1. Recognize the importance of keywords: Understand that keywords are specific words or phrases that define and categorize a book's content. They assist readers in finding relevant titles.

2. Know what qualifies as a keyword: Understand that a keyword is what readers might type into an Amazon search bar. Examples include specific topics like "ketogenic diet for women" or "how to train my puppy."

Identifying Keywords

1. Identify broad categories, subcategories, and specific topics: Break down subjects from a broad category to highly specific subjects to target your intended audience effectively.

• Broad category (e.g., cooking)

• Subcategory (e.g., international cuisine)

• Sub-subcategory (e.g., Italian cuisine)

• Specific topic (e.g., gluten-free hand-rolled gnocchi with vegan sauces)

2. Avoid overly broad or non-specific terms: Terms like "self-help" or "diet" are too broad and lack niche focus.

3. Explore Amazon's main niches: Start by searching for "Amazon book best sellers lists" and click on categories to delve deeper into specific layers, like "candlemaking."

. . .

Tools For Keyword Search

1. Use Chrome extension DS Amazon quick view: To quickly view BSR (Best Sellers Rank) on the Amazon search page.

2. Consider using KDSpy: A Chrome extension that extracts book data to analyze competition and sales figures. It's a paid tool but can save time and offer valuable insights.

Analyzing Keyword Profitability

1. Understand BSR (best sellers rank): Target keywords that have a BSR of 100,000 or less, as lower BSR signifies higher sales volume.

2. Look for keywords with reviews and revenue: Focus on keywords where books have less than 100 reviews but are generating profits. Look for at least two or three books with similar revenue, ideally $500 or more.

3. Ensure keyword relevance: Make sure that the keyword is present in the book's title to ensure relevance.

4. Use incognito window for searches: To access unbiased information free from browser biases.

5. Evaluate the demand for a keyword: Ask yourself: Are there at least three books with under 100 reviews, making at least $500 or more, and featuring the keyword in their titles? If yes, proceed; if not, explore alternative keywords.

In short, choose wisely. If the keyword doesn't meet the criteria, consider it not lucrative enough. It's vital to ensure that your selected keyword aligns with demand to avoid wasting time and effort on something that won't attract readers or generate sales.

5

ENROLLING IN KDP SELECT

What Is KDP Select?

KDP Select is a ninety-day program tailored specifically for Kindle eBooks. When you enroll in this program, you not only gain the opportunity to reach a broader audience through Amazon but also make your book accessible to Kindle Unlimited subscribers. Kindle Unlimited, Amazon's monthly reading subscription, allows its members to read all books in the catalog, including yours, for free. This unique feature enhances your reach, but it's vital to understand the commitment involved. Opting for KDP Select requires that you make your eBook exclusive to Amazon, restricting you from publishing it anywhere else on the Internet. While this exclusivity leverages the full benefits of the Kindle ecosystem, it simultaneously narrows your distribution options outside of Amazon.

KDP Select Benefits

Firstly, authors receive compensation from Amazon every time their book is borrowed and read. Every month, Amazon allocates a portion of the Kindle Unlimited subscription fees to the KDP Select Global Fund, which is then distributed among authors whose books have been borrowed and read. However, it's important to manage expectations as the earnings from this source tend to be relatively modest—usually just a few extra dollars per month.

Secondly, with KDP Select, you gain access to Kindle Countdown. This feature allows you to discount your book on a countdown clock basis. For example, if your book is usually priced at $6.99, you can offer it for $0.99 cents for one day, $1.99 the next, $2.99 the following day, and so on until the countdown expires. Kindle Countdown deals can be run for a total of five days within each ninety-day enrollment period. Being able to make your eBook free five days ever ninety-day period allows it to be seen by even more people. Some of these people may purchase the paperback, giving you a royalty, or they may claim the free eBook and end up leaving a review, both great outcomes.

Thirdly, you have access to the Free Book promotional tool. This tool enables you to offer your book for free for up to five days. Each of your Kindle books is eligible for up to five days of free book promotions once every ninety days. It's important to note that your book is not only free for Kindle Unlimited subscribers but for anyone visiting Amazon's website. Although you can offer your book for free for five consecutive days, you can choose to split those days and run the promotion for a few days at a time. Additionally, you have the flexibility to cancel the promotion if you change your mind.

Personally, I like to offer my book for a two-day free promotion, followed by a three-day free promotion about a month later. Then, I rerun the promotions in the next ninety-day cycle. It's worth mentioning that when someone downloads your book during a free promo and leaves a review, their review is classified as a "verified review," which holds more weight than an "unverified review." Reviews play a vital role in providing social proof for your book, signaling to potential readers that it is well-received and esteemed. This endorsement can enhance the book's appeal, leading to increased popularity and, consequently, more sales.

Unverified review:

Verified review:

My Thoughts

Is enrolling in KDP Select worth it? Personally, I believe so. While I can't provide concrete evidence, I have a strong belief that Amazon promotes books in this program more than those that aren't. Although there may be exceptions, it makes sense that Amazon would prioritize showcasing books in the program to a larger audience during their marketing and promotions since it benefits them as well.

Also, I have experimented with taking my books out of the program to go "wide" by uploading them to platforms like Draft2Digital, which publishes on sites such as Apple, Kobo, Barnes & Noble, and others. However, the results were underwhelming. Despite having over fifty eBooks available on those platforms, I was only making around $100-$200 per month at most. It required a significant amount of effort for minimal reward.

In this case, Pareto's 80/20 rule applies. It's important to focus on the few actions that bring the majority of results. By being exclusive to Amazon and enrolling your eBooks in the KDP Select program, you can maximize your exposure and earnings.

6

PEN NAMES

When it comes to publishing on platforms like Amazon, you are granted the liberty to choose any name you desire, whether it be your legal name or a pen name.

Let's delve into the rationale behind adopting different pen names for various genres - the art of branding. Establishing a brand is important to achieving successful book sales and fostering reader loyalty. It is the essence that draws readers back for more, eagerly anticipating your subsequent releases.

In my own case, I have meticulously crafted brands under distinct pen names, with a primary focus on educating individuals about language learning and personal finance. To preserve the integrity of each brand and avoid any confusion among my readers, I deliberately refrain from mixing the two niches with each other.

Consider the acclaimed author Stephen King, renowned for his enthralling horror novels. If he suddenly embarked on publishing historical romance novels or offering gardening tutorials, it would undoubtedly raise eyebrows. This precisely illustrates why many accomplished authors opt for multiple pen names. For instance, the celebrated J.K. Rowling, famed for the Harry Potter series, initially released "The Cuckoo's Calling" under the pseudonym Robert Galbraith. Such strategic employment of pen names enables authors to maintain a clear distinction between their diverse literary endeavors.

Managing multiple pen names on Amazon is an effortless endeavor. You retain the flexibility to create and manage multiple pen names within a single account. However, it's crucial to bear in mind that appropriating the name of a famous author, such as Steven King, as your pen name, is strictly prohibited. Furthermore, employing names or titles like "Doctor" or "PhD" requires verification by Amazon to ensure authenticity and prevent unauthorized usage.

You might wonder why someone would choose to have multiple pen names. Perhaps you start with writing finance books but later decide to delve into the world of self-help. Personally, I found myself in a similar situation. Having crafted books spanning diverse niches, I decided to have a unique pen name and brand upon each one. This decision turned out to be a good one. By accumulating customer emails from each brand, I can now effectively reach out to prior purchasers whenever I release a new book, significantly increasing the likelihood of repeat purchases. Further insights on the topic of emails will be expanded upon in chapter 17.

In the matter of selecting a pen name, I advise against expending undue effort. A mere five minutes is ample time to arrive at a suitable choice. Opt for a name that resonates with you and proceed confidently. If assistance is sought, a pen name generator such as this one can prove invaluable: https://blog. reedsy.com/pen-name-generator/

In saying all this, I also don't think it's necessary to build a brand to have a successful book. I have created several books that have gone on to do well without ever thinking about brand. But the two brands I have created I am thankful for. It makes selling future books and collecting reviews for them much easier.

7

BOOK IDEATION & OUTLINES

Setting realistic expectations for your first book is crucial. It's important to understand that it's unlikely to bring in significant earnings, and there's even a chance it may not generate any revenue at all (it's better to have low expectations and be pleasantly surprised than the other way around). However, this should not discourage you, as it is a common experience for beginners. Remember, you don't have to be exceptional right from the start. Instead, view this as an opportunity to swiftly complete your first book and move on to subsequent ones that have the potential to generate income. Adopting this mindset will bring you relief rather than disappointment, allowing you to focus on improving your skills and achieving success with your second or third book.

Now, let's delve into generating ideas for your first book. To provide an example, my own first book revolved around the topic of growing and selling Instagram accounts. I had acquired a year's worth of experience in this field and possessed a deep understanding of the process. I suggest you follow a similar approach by selecting a topic you are knowledgeable about. It could be a hobby, such as playing a musical instrument or engaging in a sport you enjoy. Alternatively, you could explore a subject related to your profession. Another idea is to write about your city and share intriguing facts about it. Additionally, if you have a unique nationality, consider exploring interesting aspects related to that. The key is to identify a subject that ignites your passion and that you possess expertise in, as this will make the writing process more enjoyable and engaging.

To inspire you further, here are some examples of books I've come across on Amazon that others have successfully published:

1. The Home Recording Studio Guide

2. Caring for Aging Parents

3. The [Your City] Travel Guide

4. Get Out of Debt - Without Increasing Your Income

5. 101 Ways Travel Improves Your Life

6. The Magic of Gluten-Free Cooking

7. Keto Diet Recipes

8. Growing Fruit Trees

9. The Solution to Stop Overthinking Your Relationship

10. Airbnb Arbitrage

11. College Hacks for Parents

12. Gut Health for Women

I hope these examples have sparked some ideas in your mind, helping you identify potential topics for your book.

Book Outlines

Creating a well-structured book outline is crucial for a smoother writing process. Think of the outline as your book's table of contents, providing a roadmap for your content. There are various styles an outline can adopt, ranging from a few lengthy chapters to several concise ones. Let's use my *Instagram Mastery* book's table of contents as an example:

1. Starting with the end in mind
2. Niche selection
3. Selecting a username
4. Ideal profile picture
5. Adding analytics
6. Optimizing your bio
7. Adding links the right way
8. Getting started
9. What to post
10. How to find accounts
11. Creating photos
12. The perfect video
13. All about stories
14. When to post
15. Ideal image sizes
16. Feed consistency
17. The perfect caption
18. What hashtags to use
19. Analyzing accounts
20. Growing your account
21. Bots and software
22. Becoming personal
23. How to contact accounts
24. How to monetize your account
25. How to do ads on other accounts
26. Bonus niches

These chapters address the twenty six most frequently asked questions I received about Instagram. Each question was transformed into a chapter, allowing me to provide detailed explanations. You can adopt a similar approach for your book, addressing common inquiries or topics of interest within your chosen subject matter. Here are some alternative ways of coming up with book outlines:

Mind Mapping

Start with a central idea or theme and branch out into subtopics or chapters.

Central idea: healthy living

- Branches:

  - Nutrition
  - Exercise
  - Mental well-being
  - Sleep habits
  - Stress management
  - Relationships

Chronological Order

If your book follows a timeline or narrative arc, organize your outline in chronological order, outlining the key events or milestones that will occur throughout the story.

Book: The History of Ancient Egypt

Chapter 1: Pre-Dynastic Period

Chapter 2: Early Dynastic Period

Chapter 3: Old Kingdom

Chapter 4: Middle Kingdom

Chapter 5: New Kingdom

Chapter 6: Late Period

Problem-Solution

Identify the main problems or challenges your book aims to address and present them as sections or chapters. Each section can then offer solutions, insights, or strategies related to the specific problem.

Book: Overcoming Procrastination

- Section 1: Understanding Procrastination

  - Chapter 1: The Psychology of Procrastination
  - Chapter 2: Identifying Procrastination Triggers

- Section 2: Strategies for Overcoming Procrastination

  - Chapter 3: Setting Clear Goals and Priorities
  - Chapter 4: Breaking Tasks into Manageable Steps

Comparative Analysis

If your book involves comparing and contrasting different concepts or ideas, structure your outline around these comparisons. Each chapter can focus on a specific comparison, providing in-depth analysis and examples.

Book: Religions of the World - A Comparative Study

- Chapter 1: Introduction to Comparative Religion
- Chapter 2: Buddhism and Hinduism: Similarities and Differences
- Chapter 3: Christianity and Islam: A Comparative Perspective
- Chapter 4: Judaism and Sikhism: Comparative Themes

Topical Organization

Divide your book into broad topics or themes. Each topic becomes a section, and within each section, you can include more specific subtopics or chapters that delve deeper into the subject matter.

Book: The Art of Photography

- Section 1: Camera Basics

- Chapter 1: Understanding Camera Types
- Chapter 2: Mastering Exposure

- Section 2: Composition and Lighting

- Chapter 3: Rule of Thirds and Framing
- Chapter 4: Natural and Artificial Lighting Techniques

. . .

Remember, these are just a few examples, and you can always combine or adapt different methods to suit your writing style and book's specific needs. The goal is to establish a clear and organized structure that guides your writing process and helps you deliver a cohesive and engaging book.

8

WRITING YOUR FIRST BOOK

Having a clear idea of what to write for your first book is essential. If your chosen topic includes a keyword, that's fantastic —it might increase the chances of generating some revenue. However, even if it doesn't, that's okay too. Consider this as a practice run, an opportunity to learn and improve.

The goal is to write 10,000 words, aiming for a minimum of 1,000 words per day over a span of ten days. Speed is the name of the game here. The objective is to complete the book as quickly as possible, allowing you to grasp the writing process and move on to your second book. With each book you write, you'll gain valuable experience, improve your skills, become faster, and grow more familiar with the process. That's the simple truth of it.

When I began my journey, I wrote nine 10,000-word books across three different niches. This provided me with ample practice and helped me gain a firm grasp of the ropes. As a bonus, one of the niches showed promising results, so I dedicated my focus to that specific area. To this day, some of those books are still selling—an incredible aspect of this business model!

Don't overthink this step. Just get it done. Start writing without getting caught up in spelling, grammar, or sentence structure concerns. Allow your thoughts to flow freely, giving them full expression on the page. Reserve meticulous editing for when you have transferred all your ideas onto paper. The key is to maintain your writing momentum. As long as the words continue to flow, keep writing.

In my personal routine, I would visit my favorite cafe every morning. With my headphones on, I would indulge in soothing classical tunes on YouTube while savoring a cup of steaming black coffee. Opening a Google Doc, I dedicated a solid ninety minutes to unleashing my thoughts onto the virtual pages. During this focused period, I refrained from opening any other browser tabs. I had two choices: embrace stillness or seize the opportunity to bring words into existence. This intentional practice became my secret to achieving a daily count of 2,000 words.

No matter if you have sixty minutes or a modest half-hour available each day, do not despair. Approach your writing sessions with intention, eliminating all distractions. By doing so, you'll be able to craft a few hundred words consistently. The key is to maintain your consistency.

Another highly effective method, although I haven't personally tried it yet, is the use of voice-to-text technology. Many authors have found success with this technique. It involves utilizing apps or features like Google Docs' "voice typing" tool to transcribe spoken words into written text. Some authors go for walks with their phones and headphones, dictating their thoughts and ideas while on the move. If you struggle to sit down and write, this method may serve as a valuable alternative for you to explore.

. . .

How Do I Find A Keyword?

Start by reflecting on your own life, considering your hobbies, interests, and daily activities. You may notice a few "how to" subjects that emerge from this list, such as guides on playing chess or the guitar. If you engage in sports or have musical interests, these themes can be combined, leading you to keywords like "how to play chess" or "how to play the guitar." There's a good chance you'll discover something relevant in this exploration. If nothing resonates, consider the hobbies and interests of those close to you. Sometimes, looking at the passions of friends or family can spark fresh ideas. Once you've identified the keyword, you're ready to dive into writing your book!

9

THE EDITING PROCESS

Congratulations on reaching a significant milestone—the completion of the first 10,000 words (or even more) of your book. This is an achievement to be proud of, but there's still work to be done before it's ready for uploading.

Editing encompasses more than just proofreading for errors; it involves reshaping and refining your manuscript as a cohesive whole. It may require reordering sections or even entire chapters to establish a seamless flow and logical progression of ideas. While I typically begin with an outline as a guide, the editing phase often calls for adjustments and reorganization to ensure optimal coherence and readability. Remember, in the journey of writing and editing, nothing is set in stone. The ability to make corrections, deletions, or additions is a tremendous advantage in the realm of self-publishing, enabling ongoing improvement.

One invaluable technique I've learned is the power of reading your work aloud during the editing process. While reviewing the text silently may seem sufficient at first, it's through the oral rendition that subtle errors and imperfections become most apparent. Nowadays, numerous free online tools are available where you can paste your chapters and have them read back to you. By engaging this feature, you can audibly experience the nuances of your writing, facilitating the identification and rectification of errors more effectively.

To further enhance the editing process, I rely on the suggested 'edits' feature in Google Docs. This initial scan helps identify and address basic errors and inconsistencies. However, for a higher degree of precision and thoroughness, I also utilize Grammarly. This comprehensive tool surpasses the capabilities of standard word processing tools, offering comprehensive error detection and insightful suggestions. By combining these editing features, I can enhance the linguistic integrity and coherence of my book, ultimately ensuring a refined and polished final product.

10

FORMATTING YOUR BOOK

<u>Font & Style</u>

To maintain a clean and visually appealing look for your books on Amazon, it's important to stick with simple fonts and styles. Not all fonts and styles translate well to Kindle, often resulting in a messy appearance after uploading. The fonts Calibri or Arial are safe bets for the text, keeping it clean and straightforward. For emphasis, utilize basic features like Bold, Italic, and bullet points. Chapter headings are set in Heading 1, while subtitles are designated as Subtitle. I prefer to use Open for paragraph spacing, ensuring a comfortable reading experience with twelve point spacing between each paragraph.

In the realm of self-publishing, employing white space between paragraphs is a favored technique, as it helps segment the content and avoids overloading the reader. For additional separation and to emphasize particular passages, consider the use of Bold or Italic formatting. A font size ranging between 10 and 12 points is typically recommended to maintain readability.

. . .

Page Breaks

Adding page breaks between chapters is essential. To insert a page break, simply position your cursor after the last word of the previous page and press ctrl + enter (command + return on mac). The text following your cursor will then move down to a new page. Continue this process throughout your book, inserting page breaks where necessary.

Note that you can easily undo page breaks by placing your cursor next to the first letter of the text and pressing the backspace key until the text returns to its original page.

Page breaks provide your Kindle book with the look and feel of traditional paper pages, preventing the text from running together. To determine where page breaks should be placed, you can refer to an actual paper book as a guide. Typically, the title, author, copyright, and table of contents each have their own page. In some cases, chapter titles have their own page, with the actual chapter contents beginning on the following page. Remember that the formatting will apply to both Kindle and paperback book files.

For my books, I insert a page break after the Title and Author page, followed by another after the Copyright page. The Table of Contents is then given its own page, followed by the Introduction and each subsequent chapter. Finally, I always include a Conclusion, an About the Author page, and a simple call to action page at the end asking for the reader to leave a review.

Book Size

Thinking about the dimensions of your book is another part of the formatting process. For non-fiction work, common sizes gravitate towards 5x8 inches or 6x9 inches, both offering good readability and portability. If you've got a book with less than

30,000 words, the 5x8 size will suit your needs. Conversely, if your manuscript approaches or surpasses 30,000 words, the 6x9 size is a more fitting choice.

Delving deeper into formatting, you'll encounter concepts like page margins and bleed. These are more advanced topics, not immediately necessary to grasp, especially if you envisage hiring a professional for these tasks. Should you opt to use software like Vellum, which I recommend, adjusting these settings becomes effortless. Their platform hosts a variety of tutorial videos, providing easy-to-follow guidance on these matters.

Has the book been helpful so far?

If what you've read so far has been helpful to you, it's likely to assist others as well. Perform a small act of kindness today—take just 30 seconds to leave a review. Your insights could serve as a beacon for someone else navigating their self-publishing journey.

Simply scan the QR code to be directed to the Amazon page, where you can effortlessly leave your valuable review.

11

CREATING YOUR KDP ACCOUNT

KDP was initially named after Kindle as it was the sole format available at the time. However, the platform has since evolved to encompass not only Kindle books but also paperbacks and hardcover editions. Despite these expansions, the platform's name has remained unchanged.

Now that our book is ready to upload we can create our KDP account. Note that you are only allowed **one** KDP account according to Amazon's terms and conditions. Making more than one can get all of your accounts terminated and permanently suspended from KDP.

You can use your Amazon shopping account to create your KDP account or you can create one from scratch with another email.

To create your account go to kdp.amazon.com/signin. Then click the yellow 'Get Started' button on the top right.

The process of setting up your KDP account might take some time as there are multiple screens to meticulously input various details. This includes important information such as your Social Security number (since, naturally, you'll have tax obligations for the income you earn through Kindle) and your bank account routing numbers (to ensure smooth direct deposits of your royalty payments every month).

Once you successfully complete the sign-up process, the KDP dashboard awaits you. You'll find four convenient tabs: Bookshelf, Reports, Community, and Marketing.

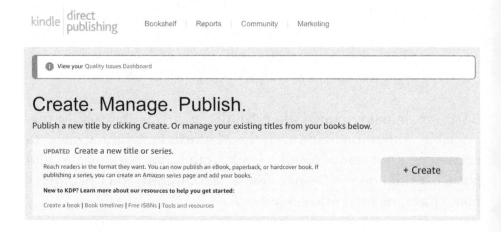

Bookshelf

This is where you will upload new books and where they will all be located. To create a new book press the large yellow '+ Create' button. You'll have a few options to choose from here: Kindle eBook, Paperback, Hardcover, and Series.

The Series feature allows you to connect books within a series, enabling readers to smoothly transition from one book to the next.

For the purpose of this book we will look at the two main types, Kindle eBook and Paperback. We will talk more about them in chapters fourteen and fifteen.

Reports

The Reports section of the KDP account is where you can track your earnings. In late 2022, Amazon made updates to this section, introducing new tabs accessible under the Reports tab. These tabs include Dashboard, Orders, KENP Read (Kindle Edition Normalized Pages Read; this will show you the page reads for the books you have enrolled in Kindle Select), Month-to-Date, Promotions, Pre-orders, and Royalties Estimator.

The joy of self-publishing lies in receiving payment for your books. Tracking sales, watching the numbers grow, and seeing your royalties increase is a rewarding experience. Amazon offers two royalty rates for Kindle eBooks: 35% or 70%. The 35% royalty option applies globally, while the 70% option applies only to designated territories including countries such as the United States, United Kingdom, Australia, and various others. The calculation for the royalty differs between the two options and can be influenced by factors like VAT, promotional pricing, and delivery costs.

For paperback books, Amazon keeps 40% and pays you 60% after deducting printing costs. Royalty income is distributed two months after the month in which it was earned, and a minimum balance of $100 is required for payment. Payments are typically made via direct deposit into your bank account on the last day of the month, varying slightly depending on the country and bank used. While the wait for payment can be frustrating, consistent sales and uploads lead to increasing earnings over time.

· · ·

Community

Within the Community tab on your KDP account page, you'll discover valuable resources. This includes Amazon announcements and forums where publishers can seek advice and share knowledge. While the forums may be challenging for newcomers, reading posts can be educational. Additionally, the Amazon HELP section, accessible from the Community page, provides comprehensive answers to account-related queries. This page houses a wealth of tutorials and user guides covering every aspect of the KDP site.

For direct assistance, the Contact Us link can be found under the Help tab within the Community section, which directs you to relevant information before reaching out to Amazon.

Marketing

The Marketing tab on your KDP account page offers various resources.

KDP Select: Enroll eBooks in KDP Select to make them eligible for promotional opportunities.

Amazon ads: Access the Amazon advertising portal for effective book marketing campaigns.

Author central: Manage your author central page to view books, sales ranks, and customer reviews from one convenient portal.

A+ content: Utilize A+ content to enhance product detail pages with images, text, and comparison tables, providing readers with more engaging and informative buying experiences.

Run a price promotion: Utilize Kindle Select to create Kindle Countdown Deals and Free Book promotions, either through the Bookshelf page or directly within your book's listing.

Nominate your eBooks: Participate in Amazon contests and special promotions by nominating your eBooks for Kindle Deals, which offer limited-time discounts, or for Prime Reading, where select eBooks are available for free to Prime Members.

12

FORMATTING YOUR BOOK FILES FOR UPLOAD

There are four main methods to format and prepare your book files for uploading onto Amazon's platform. They are: formatting in Word, utilizing Kindle Create, using Vellum, or hiring a professional formatter.

Formatting In Word

After formatting the content of your book document, you can upload it directly to Amazon in the Web Page Filtered format (.DOCX). To save your book as a Web Page Filtered document, select the "Save As" option and choose the desired location on your computer. This approach provides flexibility for editing and updating your book files, but it has limited formatting capabilities and may not result in a professional appearance.

Formatting In Kindle Create

Kindle Create is a free book formatting software provided by Amazon. It supports both Kindle eBooks and paperback books. After downloading Kindle Create, open the program and select your .DOCX book file to upload. Kindle Create offers various optional features to enhance your book, such as a clickable table of contents and formatting options for chapter titles and subtitles. You can experiment with these features and make changes as needed before publishing.

Formatting In Vellum

Vellum, a well-known book formatting program found at Vellum.com, is highly regarded among authors. It offers a range of advanced features such as custom drop caps, ornamental flourishes, box sets, and formatting options for various platforms. Although it comes with a price tag ($199 one-time payment at the time of this writing), Vellum provides unparalleled flexibility and customization, giving your book a polished and professional appearance similar to industry giants.

Hiring A Professional Formatter

If you find formatting overwhelming, you can hire a professional formatter from platforms like Fiverr or Upwork. These platforms offer a range of formatting services at different price points. When hiring, review the seller's feedback, read their service description, and consider the number of revisions offered.

Ensuring your book files are appropriately formatted for upload is a crucial step in the self-publishing journey. Don't be discouraged by it, as it's a manageable task whether you choose to do it yourself or seek professional help. In my case, I've found great value in using Vellum. If you're committed to publishing and plan on doing it long-term, investing in and mastering Vellum is worthwhile. It significantly speeds up the publishing process by eliminating the need for back-and-forth communication with freelancers during formatting. Plus, in the long run, it proves to be a cost-effective solution. It's worth noting that Vellum is exclusively available for Mac users, but you can access it on a PC through the cloud.

13

CREATING BOOK COVERS

When it comes to selling books on Amazon, the significance of book covers can't be overstated. Contrary to popular belief, people do judge a book by its cover and potential customers will base their decision to click on a book by its visual appeal. Customers have nothing else to judge their decision off of, so they will go with the information they have, which is the cover. In this chapter, we will explore a few methods for creating book covers suitable for both Kindle and paperback formats: designing your own covers using graphic design software, hiring a professional designer, or hiring a professional design company to create you one.

Before delving into these options, it's important to understand some key aspects of book covers on Amazon. Kindle eBook covers must adhere to specific requirements set by Amazon, including a recommended height/width ratio of 1.6:1, a minimum image height of 2,500 pixels for high-definition devices, and cover files with dimensions of 2,560 x 1,600 pixels. The file size can not exceed 50MB. Additionally, it's crucial to avoid copyright infringement, pricing information, or temporary promotions on the cover.

Design Your Own Book Cover Using Graphic Design Software

This route is suitable if you possess design skills or are willing to learn, especially if this is one of your initial books and you view it as an opportunity to practice rather than expecting significant profits. Two popular options for graphic design software are Adobe Photoshop and Canva.com. I recommend Canva as it often offers a free trial and is more user-friendly compared to Photoshop. You can find helpful tutorials on YouTube to learn the basics of image design and get started on crafting your cover.

Hire A Professional Designer

If you're serious about building a successful book-selling business, it's a smart move to hire a skilled designer to create your book covers. Platforms like Fiverr and Upwork offer convenient opportunities to post job listings or search for freelancers specializing in book cover design. These platforms provide portfolios and examples of previous work, making it easier to find a designer who understands different genres and can attract potential readers. By searching for "book cover designer," you'll find a wide range of freelancers to choose from.

In the beginning, I would recommend starting with Fiverr, as it allows for a quick and easy start. You can browse through profiles, check out the artists' previous creations, and if you find a style you like and consider it high quality, you can purchase their service, provide the necessary details, and they'll get started. While some designers offer their services for as low as $5 per illustration, it's important to note that the quality may not always be the highest. However, as a starting point, I suggest purchasing services from three or four different $5 designers, identifying what you like from each of them, and then ask one designer to combine those elements into a single cover. With an investment of around $20, you can obtain a beautiful cover.

As your business grows, you'll want to level up and have a dedicated designer who truly understands your vision. Upwork is a better platform for this, as it allows for direct and efficient communication. Over time, you can establish a relationship with a specific designer who can cater to your needs. Personally, I now have my own designer whom I can message at any time, and they usually get back to me within a day or two with a high quality, unique cover design, thanks to the rapport we've built. Currently, I pay them $50 per cover.

Hire A Professional Design Company

Numerous design companies out there specialize in crafting fantastic book covers. My personal choice was a service called 100 Covers. Their skilled designers produce quality, affordable covers for $100 and, with a quick Google search for "100 Covers discount code," you can often find a deal and get the price down to $50! They have a decent turnaround time of about one to two weeks and offer unlimited revisions as well. So, you could order the cover right after you finalize your book's topic and title, meaning while you're busy penning the book, your cover design is also in progress. By the time you've put down your last word, your cover should be ready too. This is an excellent and cost-effective solution if you're not ready to invest in design skills or hire a professional just yet.

. . .

Paperback Covers

For paperback books, the cover file should include the front cover, spine, and back cover in a single PDF image. The image size depends on the book's page count and trim size. Amazon provides a convenient free Paperback file setup calculator and cover templates, which can be accessed through this link: https://kdp.amazon.com/en_US/cover-calculator.

Converting an eBook cover into a paperback one can be cost-efficient and relatively simple. You have the option to leverage platforms like Fiverr.com, where for just $5, you can hire someone to accomplish the task. Another alternative is to utilize Canva.com; you can download the mentioned template and take on the creation of the spine and back cover yourself. This DIY route or employing economical online services typically turns out to be more affordable than engaging a professional designer or a design company.

Before I found my own designer, I found an efficient balance by employing 100Covers for the creation of the cover at the reasonable price of $50, and then personally designing the spine and back cover. This approach saved not only money but also valuable time. It reduced the need for communication on Fiverr and expedited the process, ensuring a more efficient workflow.

What Is A Good Book Cover?

To fully appreciate the nuances of the following images, consider scanning the QR code located at the back of the book. Once you've entered your details, I'll zip a colorful PDF your way, enabling you to visually understand the ingredients that cook up a best-selling book cover. Crafting a stand-out book cover is an art that combines diverse elements, but there are a handful of golden rules that consistently remain relevant:

1. Theme Alignment: Your cover should visually embody the essence of your book's content. Think of it as a pictorial summary of your book.

2. Clear and Readable Title: Select a large, legible font with a color contrast that stands out. The title should be instantly readable, even from a quick glance.

3. Professional Appearance: A well-crafted, professional-looking cover signals to the reader that they're in for a quality read. Don't underestimate the power of first impressions!

4. Scroll-Stopping Power: This is the real challenge, but it's also where the magic happens. Your cover needs to be so striking that it makes browsers stop in their tracks and click to learn more. It's not easy, but the possibilities are virtually limitless.

Let's dive into a fun activity and try to decode these book covers, without peeking at their titles:

Starting with the one on the far left, what's your best guess? Pay attention to the elements on the cover, what story do they seem to tell? Moving to the middle one, can you identify the types of food displayed on the cover? And as for the cover on the far right, what's your hunch? Flip to the next page to see if you were right!

  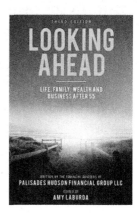

Without even taking a look at the titles, you could probably make some educated guesses about the first two covers. The leftmost one is buzzing with honey-themed elements, so it's likely related to honey production. For the middle cover, the sight of cookies and brownies might have tipped you off that it's a cookbook or a baking guide. The last cover, though, doesn't give away much. There's nothing on it to suggest that the book is about finance. Both the image and title fall short in that regard, making it a less effective cover.

The full titles of the covers are:

Beekeeping for Beginners: The New Complete Guide to Raise a Healthy and Thriving Beehive

100 Cookies: The Baking Book for Every Kitchen, with Classic Cookies, Novel Treats, Brownies, Bars, and More

Looking Ahead: Life, Family, Wealth And Business After 55

Ready for another round? This time, choose between the left and right cover – which one grabs your attention more? Make your pick before peeking at the answer below.

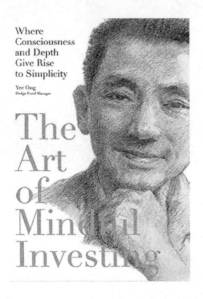
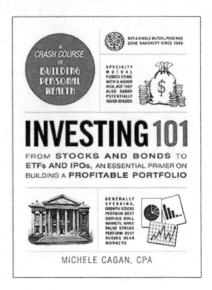

If your pick was the right one, then you're spot on! Both books delve into the world of investing, but the cover on the right successfully incorporates symbols of finance and investment. Plus, it's definitely more of a feast for the eyes compared to the one on the left.

Now, take a look at this template cover – once a hit, it's now been so overused by self-publishers that it might as well have "amateur" written all over it. You'd want to steer clear of such designs to keep your work from blending into the crowd.

Beneath, you'll spot several covers that have used this same template under the keyword "Puppy training for beginners." A couple of them manage to break the mold though. Can you spot the standouts?

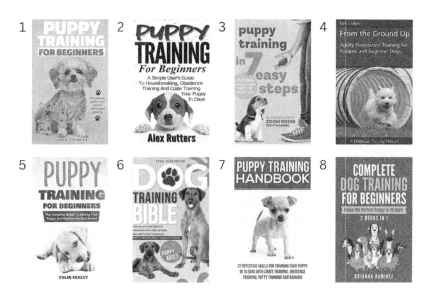

Answer on the next page.

Did you pick out numbers three and six? Bravo! These covers certainly break away from the pack and shine in their unique light. Objectively speaking, they outperform the rest, plus, their Best Seller Rank (BSR) on Amazon confirms they're selling well!

Best-Selling Book Covers

Feast your eyes on some best-selling covers. Use them as a springboard for ideas and inspiration as you craft your own masterpiece.

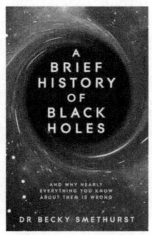
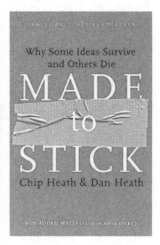

See how beautifully the cover image marries with the book topic? It feels organic and it elevates the whole book.

Final Thoughts

Against common sayings, yes, people indeed judge a book by its cover. After investing your heart and soul into birthing your book, the last thing you want is to cut corners on the cover. To shine brightly in the vast Amazon galaxy, your book needs a professionally polished, attention-grabbing cover. A visually enticing cover can shift the scales in your favor. And as you wade deeper into the publishing waters, you'll develop an instinct for spotting fantastic covers, understanding their magic, and collaborating with a designer to whip up a cover that fits your niche like a glove.

14

UPLOADING YOUR EBOOK

Uploading your book to Amazon is the easiest step in the self-publishing journey, whether you're publishing it as a Kindle eBook or a paperback. It's easier than writing the book itself, formatting it, or even promoting it. Once you've created your KDP account, it will only take a few minutes to upload your book.

To begin the process of uploading your book to Amazon, log into your KDP account. After signing in, you'll find yourself on your personal KDP page. At the top of the page, you'll see several tabs: Bookshelf, Reports, Community, and Marketing. The page defaults to your Bookshelf, which is the perfect place for uploading new books.

In large type, you'll see the words "Create. Manage. Publish." Below that text, there's a field titled "Create a new title or series." Here, Amazon informs you that you can reach readers in various formats, such as eBooks, paperbacks, hardcovers, and Kindle Vella stories. If you're publishing a series, you can create an Amazon series page and add your books.

Let's start with uploading a Kindle book. Click on the yellow "+ Create" button. This action will open a new page titled "What would you like to create?" Inside the Kindle eBook square, click on the yellow "Create eBook" button. This will bring up a new screen consisting of three separate pages.

The first page is titled "Kindle eBook Details" and it contains several sections that need to be completed.

Language

The first field you'll encounter is for Language, and it's tailored to match the language of the Amazon site you're registered under. For example, if you're publishing in America, the default language will be English. Nonetheless, you also have the fantastic option of releasing your books in other languages, such as Afrikaans, Arabic, Danish, Dutch, Finnish, French, German, Italian, Japanese, Portuguese, Spanish, Swedish, and more.

As you venture further into your self-publishing journey, exploring the possibility of translating and publishing your books in multiple languages could prove immensely beneficial, as it opens up opportunities to connect with a broader audience. Personally, I decided to translate my best-selling book into Spanish, German, and French. While the Spanish and German versions have steadily sold a few copies each month, the French version has exceeded all expectations, becoming my fourth best-selling book this year!

However, a word of advice: I'd recommend considering this step once you have a solid foundation of at least ten books published and a consistent income of at least $1,000 per month. Translations can be quite costly and trying new markets involves some risk. So, it's best to be well-prepared before taking the leap.

. . .

Book Title

The next field is for your book title. Here, you'll need to provide the main title of your book and, if applicable, a subtitle. It's important to note that while you can change your Kindle book titles at any time after publication, you cannot change your paperback book titles. Additionally, your paperback title and subtitle must match your cover design exactly for Amazon to publish your book. However, your Kindle and paperback book titles don't necessarily have to match. To make things simple, come up with **one** title that has the main keywords for both Kindle and paperback. Paste it into the main title box with a '-' in between the title and subtitle i.e. The Ketogenic Cook Book - A Beginner's Guide To Learning The Keto Diet

Book Title	Enter your title as it appears on the book cover. This field cannot be changed after your book is published. Learn more about book titles.
	Book Title
	The Ketogenic Cook Book - A Beginner' Guide To Learning The Keto Diet
	Subtitle (Optional)

Series

If your book is part of a series, you have the option to add series details to help readers easily find your other titles on a single detail page. You can either add the title you're uploading to an existing series or create a new series. Once the setup is complete, any linked formats for the title will automatically be added to the series. This allows readers to view all available formats for your series titles on one page and select the format that suits them best.

Creating a series also enables you to establish a reading order for your audience. You can number the titles for a linear reading experience or leave them unordered for readers to enjoy in any order they prefer. When creating a series, make sure to include books with common characteristics like characters, settings, or chronology, as it helps readers understand what to expect from your series and allows for easy grouping of related titles.

In case you have different language versions of your series titles, it's recommended to create separate series for each language. This ensures that readers can easily find all the titles in your series within their preferred language.

Avoid adding duplicate content to the same series, as readers purchasing all the titles expect unique content for each book (if it's not unique, they may leave a negative review).

In the beginning of your journey, you won't have a series and shouldn't even be thinking about this so don't worry too much about it.

Edition Number

In the edition number field, you have the option to specify the edition of your book. If your book is the first edition or a new edition of an existing book, you can enter the appropriate edition number. For instance, if you initially published your book and then made significant revisions or updates to create a new version, you can indicate it as the second edition. It's important to note that the edition number is not mandatory.

From my personal experience, I would recommend publishing a new version instead of revisiting and updating an old one. By doing so, you'll have two separate listings, doubling your earning potential. This approach is particularly beneficial for books that have titles like "The 2023 Cookbook" and "The 2024 Cookbook" (note this is an example and creating a cookbook is not recommended at all).

Author

In the author field, you enter the first name and last name of the primary author or contributor of the book. This can be your own legal name or a pen name. It's important to note that the author's name cannot be changed once the book is published on Kindle or paperback.

Contributors

If there are additional contributors to your book, such as co-authors, editors, illustrators, or translators, you can add their names under the contributors section. You can specify their roles, such as author, editor, illustrator, introduction, narrator, photographer, preface, or translator. It's important to note that if you are the author of the book, you only need to enter your name in the author section and not again under contributors.

Description

The description section is crucial as it provides a summary of your book that entices customers to make a purchase. You can use HTML code or Amazon's formatting features to enhance the description. This includes adding bold, italic, underline, numbers, bullets, and paragraphs. When writing your book description, Amazon suggests keeping it simple, compelling, and professional. Focus on describing the main plot, theme, or idea without overwhelming or confusing potential readers. Use short and easy-to-scan sentences within a 150-word paragraph. Grab readers' attention with a memorable first sentence and clearly indicate the genre of your book. Ensure your description is polished with no misspellings or grammatical errors, and consider seeking feedback from others to refine it.

Although Amazon imposes restrictions on certain content in descriptions, such as offensive material, personal contact information, reviews or testimonials, time-sensitive information, and promotional material, successful authors have a self-publishing secret up their sleeves. By loading your description with relevant keywords, you can increase the chances of potential readers discovering your book. But here's the trick: rather than simply listing keywords, incorporate them into sentences that make the description engaging and informative.

Suppose your book is about healthy eating and plant-based diets. You can create a captivating sentence for your book description like this: "Ready to transform your health and embrace a vibrant lifestyle? Explore the world of nutritious plant-based eating and discover how to nourish your body with delicious and wholesome meals!" Remember, the first four lines of your description play a crucial role as they are visible to customers prior to clicking on "read more." Make sure those lines are enticing and consider using a bold font to make them stand out.

Publishing Rights

You have two options in the Publishing Rights section. If you own the copyright and hold the necessary publishing rights for the content, select the first option. This is applicable when you have written the book yourself; and under US copyright law, your work is protected as soon as you create it. You are the sole owner and can publish it without any formal agreement with a publisher. The second option, "This is a public domain work," is chosen when you are translating a book that is already available for free on Amazon.

Until your book is making multiple thousand dollars a month, you don't need to worry about getting your book copyrighted. It costs money and takes months to do. In regards to public domain work, this isn't a viable way to create a long lasting brand or make money so don't go down this path.

Keywords

When it comes to adding keywords to your books on the "backend," there are a couple of things to consider for better results. The title and subtitle may have their limits, but Amazon provides an opportunity to add more keywords. Here, we have two approaches to choose from: either use one keyword in each box or stuff the boxes with multiple words.

Someone in the publishing community did a test to see which approach works best. Turns out, having fewer words in each box gives more weight to those words compared to cramming multiple words in one box. To me, it makes sense to go with one word per box. If you've crafted a good title and subtitle, you shouldn't need to add multiple keywords in each box. Plus, don't forget to include them in your book description. If you have any leftovers, you can throw them in the additional boxes provided (you get seven of them).

To find these keywords, pay attention to the suggestions that pop up in Amazon's search field dropdown. Put yourself in the shoes of a reader and think about how they would search for a book. You can also check out the keywords used in other popular books in your genre and add relevant ones to your list.

Amazon has a few keyword types they don't recommend using. These include stuff that's already in your book's metadata (like the title and contributors), subjective claims about how awesome your book is (like calling it the "best novel ever"), time-sensitive statements ("new," "on sale," "available now"), common info for most books in the category (like "book"), spelling mistakes, and different versions of spacing, punctuation, capitalization, and plurals. Also, don't use Amazon program names like "Kindle Unlimited" or "KDP Select" as keywords.

We want to build a business that lasts, so it's better to play it safe. By optimizing your title, description, and keywords, you can make your book easier to find on Amazon and increase your chances of reaching the right readers.

Categories

Picking the perfect categories for your book is super important too. When setting up your Kindle eBook and paperback versions, you get to choose three categories for each. But here's the kicker: the categories available are different for Kindle eBooks and paperbacks. This actually works in your favor because you can pick different categories for each version right from the get-go. By doing this, you increase your book's visibility across multiple places which leads to more eyeballs, and more opportunities for book sales.

Age & Grade Range

When it comes to the "age and grade range" section, it is optional and typically used for children's books, allowing parents to sort books by age. If you're publishing books for adults, you can bypass this section.

Pre-Orders

Regarding pre-orders, they are common for fiction writers as they build a fan base eagerly anticipating their next release, especially those in a series, encouraging readers of the first book to pre-order the second one. Some authors even load several books in a series as pre-orders, particularly if they release new books every month or two. If your books are part of a series, Amazon will automatically notify readers about the next book, whether it's on pre-order or already available. For pre-order options, select either "I am ready to release my book now" or "Make my Kindle eBook available for Pre-order." It's important to note that paperback books cannot be put up for pre-order. If you're offering both a Kindle and paperback version, it's advisable to upload the paperback a few days before the scheduled Kindle release, as Amazon's approval process for paperbacks may take longer.

For non-fiction books, you don't usually use pre-orders. I've never done it, and some publishing friends who have tried said they didn't see much of a difference. That's great for us as it's one less thing to worry about.

Second page

After completing the first page of KDP, you can choose to save as a draft or save and continue, which will take you to the second page for uploading your manuscript. It's worth noting that most of the information can be changed before publishing, except for specific fields like the Kindle book title and the author's name. It's crucial to double-check and ensure the accuracy of the entered information. Now let's move on to the next step in the publishing process.

Digital Rights Management

According to Amazon, DRM (Digital Rights Management) is a feature specifically designed to prevent unauthorized distribution of your Kindle book file. However, it's worth noting that some authors opt not to apply DRM to their books, as they may intentionally encourage readers to share their work.

Should you choose to enable DRM, rest assured that customers will still have the ability to lend the book to another user for a limited period or purchase it as a gift from the Kindle store. It is essential to be aware that once your book is published, you cannot modify its DRM setting.

Personally, I prefer to leave the DRM box unchecked, as it is the default option. Amazon likely has valid reasons for such a choice. It's important to recognize that determined individuals who intend to illicitly acquire your book will find ways to do so, regardless of DRM measures. Therefore, attempting to impede such actions may prove futile.

Upload Book Manuscript

The next step is to upload your book manuscript. Depending on how you created your file, whether in Word (.DOCX), using Kindle Create, Vellum, or with the assistance of someone else, you can simply click on the yellow button and select the file from your computer. It's important to remember that you can upload a new version of your book at any time. If Amazon detects a spelling error in your manuscript file, an alert will be displayed. You can click on the potential spelling error to determine if it is indeed a mistake or if it's unrecognized slang. If it's a genuine error, you can make the necessary corrections in your Word document, reformat the file in Kindle Create, and then upload the updated version. If the word is not a spelling error, you can simply click the "ignore" button.

. . .

Kindle eBook Cover

Moving on, the next field requires you to upload your book's cover. Amazon provides two options in this section: you can either launch the Cover Creator tool, which allows you to create a cover using Amazon's templates or your own image with overlaid text (which you should **never** do), or you can upload a cover you already have in JPG or TIFF format. We will explore these options more extensively later, but for now, remember that this is where you will upload your cover file. It's important to upload all the necessary files before proceeding to the third and final page of the listing form.

After your manuscript and cover files have undergone processing, you'll be required to click on the "launch previewer" option to review and give your approval for the files. It's important to keep in mind that Amazon might take a while to process these files, sometimes taking up to ten or twenty minutes. Therefore, if you experience this delay, rest assured that it is entirely normal.

ISBN

An ISBN, which stands for International Standard Book Number, is an important identifier for books. While Kindle eBooks do not require an ISBN, it is mandatory for paperback books. The decision to purchase ISBNs becomes crucial if you intend to self-publish your books on platforms other than Amazon. Although obtaining ISBNs can be costly, it grants you full control over your publications.

Personally, if I was starting again, I wouldn't bother thinking about purchasing ISBNs and going wide. The majority of your sales will be coming from Amazon so it's better to put your focus there (remember the 80/20 rule?). The extra effort, time and money of uploading your book to other platforms and the cost of the ISBN's isn't worth it. Just use Amazon's free ISBN they provide, publish your book, and then move onto making your next one.

Third page

Once you have approved your book and cover files, you can save your progress and continue to the third and final page. It's important to note that you can change the information on this page, including the book files, at any time.

<u>KDP Select Enrollment</u>

At the top of the third and final page, you will find the KDP Select enrollment section. We spoke about this earlier (chapter five) but here is a quick recap of what it is. Kindle Select is Amazon's Kindle Unlimited program. Kindle Unlimited allows Amazon customers to pay a monthly subscription fee to access and borrow eligible Kindle books. To make your book available for Kindle Unlimited subscribers to read for free, you must voluntarily enroll it in the KDP Select program. Traditionally published books are rarely enrolled in KDP Select, as it primarily consists of self-published works. Under the KDP Select program, Amazon collects the Kindle Unlimited subscription fees and distributes the revenue among the authors whose books were downloaded by Kindle Unlimited subscribers. As of the time of writing, the payout is approximately half a cent per page read, meaning authors earn around one penny for every two pages read. It's important to note that Amazon counts page-reads based on physical page turns by the reader, so authors are no longer paid for skipped pages.

When it comes to enrolling your Kindle books in KDP Select, publishers have the option to enroll for a ninety-day period. You can choose to renew automatically or manually re-enroll by turning off the automatic renewal option.

This isn't the reason we're signing up for for KDP Select however. When you enroll in KDP Select, you get two other benefits:

Opportunity to run free book promotions: You can run promotions where your book is available for free for up to five days per book during each ninety-day enrollment period. Your book will be shown to more people, leading to more paperback sales or reviews from people reading the eBook.

Opportunity to run Kindle countdown deals: You can also run Kindle Countdown Deals for books priced between $2.99 and $24.99. This allows you to offer your book at a discounted price for a limited time, creating a sense of urgency for potential buyers.

When you decide to enroll your Kindle book in KDP Select, it comes with a condition of remaining exclusive to Amazon for a period of ninety days. This exclusivity requirement solely applies to the eBook version of your book, preventing you from publishing it on other distribution platforms. However, you are free to publish the paperback version of your book on alternative platforms.

In my view, it's advisable to have your book enrolled in the KDP Select program for at least the initial ninety days. It stands to reason that Amazon would prioritize and promote books within its own program over those that aren't. While it's not to say that success is impossible without enrollment, opting for the ninety-day exclusivity increases the likelihood of your book gaining traction and achieving success, in my opinion.

. . .

Territories

Moving on to the Territories section, Amazon provides the option to make your book available worldwide or select individual territories. Simply select "All territories (worldwide rights)." This allows customers from various Amazon websites, including the US, UK, Germany, France, Spain, Italy, Japan, Netherlands, Brazil, Mexico, Canada, India, Australia, and more, to purchase your book.

Primary Marketplace

In the Primary Marketplace section, you have the opportunity to select the main website where you anticipate the majority of your book sales will take place. If it's not already set to Amazon.com for the United States, I recommend making that adjustment. In all likelihood, around 95% of your sales will come from this marketplace, as has been the case for me as well.

Pricing, Royalty & Distribution

As an author, you have the freedom to set the price of your books on Amazon and they offer different royalty options based on price and delivery method.

For books priced between 99 cents and $2.98, or those priced at $10 or more, you can opt for a 35% payout. This option doesn't incur a delivery fee, making it suitable for lower-priced or large file size books. To maximize sales, I recommend setting your book at 99 cents for the first month.

On the other hand, books priced between $2.99 and $9.99, which is the majority range for Kindle eBooks, can earn a 70% payout. This option does have a delivery fee of 15 cents per megabyte. Once the initial thirty days have passed, I suggest increasing the eBook price to $2.99.

Keep in mind that pricing strategies may vary depending on factors like genre, book length, and perceived value. When distributing your book internationally through Amazon, they automatically convert the price based on the local currency. You can refer to the Pricing, Royalty, and Distribution section for a chart illustrating your share of royalties at different price points. Remember, you can adjust your book's pricing at any time.

Regarding KDP Select enrollment and pricing, my strategy has evolved over time. Initially, I priced my Kindle books at $2.99 and enrolled them in KDP Select. However, as I started writing longer non-fiction books, I raised the price to $9.99 and removed them from KDP Select. It's worth noting that with outright purchases on Amazon, authors receive payment regardless of whether the customer reads the book. Even years later, I still earn page-read royalties from readers who downloaded my books during their time in KDP Select.

For your first book, launching it at 99 cents under the 30% royalty level can be beneficial. This lower price may boost sales and help you gather reviews, which are crucial for book visibility and future sales. Remember, you can always adjust the price later as your book gains traction. If you don't have a substantial social media following, enrolling your first book in KDP Select and allowing it to be borrowed by Kindle Unlimited members can be a good strategy. Although earnings per page read are minimal, the borrows can potentially generate reviews and improve your book's ranking. As a new author, initial readers may choose to borrow rather than purchase your book, so their reviews are important for future sales.

To encourage readers to leave reviews, consider including a friendly note at the end of your book. Politely request reviews and provide a QR code (you can make one for free on Canva.com) that directs them straight to the review page. Amazon also prompts readers to leave reviews and directs them to the book's detail page, but a personal request can be effective.

It's common for new authors to hesitate when pricing their books too low, feeling that their work deserves higher prices. However, it's important to recognize the highly competitive nature of the Kindle market, with numerous self-published authors vying for readers' attention. Many of these authors have been publishing for years. As an experienced Kindle eBook author since 2019, I found that it took time and a growing readership before I could justify pricing my Kindle eBooks at $9.99.

Book Lending

With book lending there is the ability for users to lend digital books purchased from the Kindle Store to their loved ones. Each book can be lent once for a period of fourteen days, during which the lender temporarily forfeits access to the book. It's important to note that book lending is exclusive to Kindle books bought on Amazon.

If you have purchased a copy of your own book, you do have the privilege to lend it. However, be aware that the terms of the Kindle Book Lending program allow only one loan per title, and such loans do not generate royalty payments.

By default, all titles under KDP are enrolled in lending. Nonetheless, for titles under the 35% royalty option, you have the flexibility to opt-out of lending during the title setup process by deselecting the checkbox in the "Book Lending" section. Keep in mind that opting out is not possible for titles under the 70% royalty option or titles included in the lending program of another sales or distribution channel.

Speaking from personal experience, I no longer allow lending of my books. While I initially enabled it, I discovered that book lending is not as popular as it once was. Therefore, my preference now lies in having readers either borrow my books under KDP Select or outright purchase them, allowing me to generate income.

Publishing Your eBook

When the time comes to publish your Kindle eBook, make sure all the necessary sections are properly filled out. Then, you'll find the orange "Publish Your Kindle eBook" button waiting for you at the bottom of the page. Please be aware that it may take up to seventy-two hours for Amazon to make your Kindle eBook available on their website. The good news is that you can make changes to most of the fields even after publication.

15

UPLOADING YOUR PAPERBACK

Creating Your Paperback

To create a paperback version of your book, the process is similar to uploading the Kindle version. Once your Kindle eBook is published, it will appear on the Bookshelf in your KDP account. Click on the "+ Create paperback" link to begin.

If you have already uploaded a Kindle version of the book you wish to turn into a paperback, some fields will be automatically pre-filled for your convenience. However, you always have the option to make edits to most of them. One field that differs from the Kindle page is the Adult Content section. Here, you will be asked whether the book contains language, situations, or images that may not be suitable for children under eighteen years old. You can select either NO or YES. Unless your book is explicitly intended for children, it is recommended to choose NO.

After clicking the "Save & Continue" button on the first page, you will be guided to the second page where you can provide further details about your paperback book. Unlike eBooks, printed books require an ISBN. You can either purchase ISBNs from

Bowker.com or opt for Amazon's free KDP ISBN (just use the Amazon's free one for now).

When it comes to the Publication Date field, if your book has previously been published on another platform, enter the date of its initial publication (just mentioning this so you know why it's there). However, if this is your book's first-ever publication, feel free to skip this section, as the date will automatically be filled in once your book goes live on Amazon's website. It's worth noting that paperback books cannot be submitted for pre-order, as that option is only available for Kindle books.

Paperback Options

Paperback books offer various options for the page interiors. Amazon provides the following Ink and Paper Types:

- Black and white interior with cream paper (typically used for fiction and memoirs, with a paper weight of 55 pounds).
- Black and white interior with white paper (Amazon's default selection and commonly used for nonfiction, with a paper weight of 55 pounds).
- Standard color interior with white paper (a more affordable option for books with color, although not recommended for those with full-color page elements, with a paper weight of 55 pounds).
- Premium color interior with white paper (suitable for books with full-color elements like illustrations, graphics, and images, with a paper weight of 60 pounds).

Trim Size: The trim size refers to the dimensions of the pages in your paperback book. Amazon offers a range of sizes, with 5x8 inches or 6x9 inches being the most common for non-fiction self-published books.

Bleed Settings: Bleed refers to printing at or off the edge of a page to support images and illustrations. Most books use "no bleed" unless there is a specific need for it.

Paperback Cover Finish: Amazon offers two options for the finish of your paperback book cover: glossy and matte. The glossy finish provides a shiny appearance that enhances black covers and artwork while the matte cover finish offers a subtle, polished look with minimal sheen. There's no right or wrong here, you can choose whichever you like. I personally do matte for all of my books as it gives a premium feel in the hands.

Manuscript: In this section, you will upload the file for your paperback book. Amazon supports various file formats, including PDF, DOC, DOCX, HTML, and RTF.

Book Cover: Here, you upload your own print-ready PDF file. It's important to note that the paperback book cover is different from the Kindle version, as it includes a spine and back cover in addition to the front cover.

Launch Preview: After uploading your manuscript and cover, you can click the Launch Previewer button. Amazon will process the uploads, which may take some time. Before moving on to the final page, it's essential to preview and accept the complete file of your book.

Summary: On the second page of the book listing, you will find the Summary section, displaying the complete file of your book, including the cover and interior pages as they will appear in print. Amazon will also show you the printing cost, which will be deducted automatically from the sale price of your book. Once you have reviewed and approved the file, you can proceed to the third and final page.

Third Page

On the third page of the publishing process, you will encounter the Territories section, similar to what you experienced when uploading the Kindle version of your book. Here, you can decide whether to make your paperback book available worldwide (with worldwide rights) or select specific regions. You should always select worldwide rights to maximize your book's reach.

The Primary Marketplace field determines the primary marketplace where your book will be available. By default, it will be set to the country you are uploading from. For instance, if you're uploading from the United States, the default will be Amazon.com. No matter where you live you should make your default Amazon.com as that's where most sales come from.

Pricing, Royalty, & Distribution

Publishers earn a 60% royalty for paperback books. This royalty is calculated after deducting Amazon's share of the purchase price and the printing cost. The printing cost varies depending on factors like the number of pages and trim size of your book.

While international buyers will see the price you set for your book, it's important to note that paperback books are not as widely distributed as Kindle eBooks.

Publish Your Paperback Book

After setting the price for your paperback book, you can click on the "Publish your paperback book" button to make it available on Amazon's website. Unlike Kindle eBooks, which are typically approved within a day, paperback books may take several days to be approved. This is because Amazon meticulously checks each paperback to ensure it will print correctly when ordered, ensuring a high-quality reading experience for customers.

Request Proof Copies

Once your paperback book is successfully published, you have the option to request proof copies at a discounted rate. This allows you to physically review the book and make any necessary adjustments before making it available for purchase. Alternatively, you can order copies directly from the Amazon website, which not only benefits your author rank but also allows you to earn royalties from the sales of those copies.

16

AUDIOBOOKS

In the continuously evolving landscape of the publishing industry, audiobooks have emerged as a game-changer. They offer an engaging and flexible format that appeals to today's always-on-the-go society. Creating and uploading your content on platforms such as Audible allows you to tap into this burgeoning market, vastly increasing your potential audience. Not only do audiobooks make literature accessible to those who may have reading difficulties or visual impairments, but they also provide an alternative for individuals who prefer auditory learning or those who simply wish to consume content while commuting, exercising, or carrying out daily chores. Furthermore, with a rise in the use of digital technology and smartphones, the process of accessing audiobooks has become more effortless than ever. By stepping into the realm of audiobooks, you open your work up to these numerous benefits, amplifying your reach and influence as an author.

Where Should I Begin with Audiobook Creation?

The audiobook market is primarily dominated by Audible, making it the ideal platform for your audiobook debut. Keeping in line with the 80/20 rule, focusing on Audible can effectively cater to most of your audiobook audience. However, instead of audible.com, authors should turn their attention to ACX.com first. Once you create an account there, you can claim your books from Amazon and kickstart your audiobook journey.

ACX.com also serves as a great marketplace to find your ideal narrator. I've worked with narrators whose rates range from $40 to several hundred dollars per finished hour. What does 'per finished hour' mean, you ask? It's essentially the cost of one hour of polished, narrated audio. Though the actual reading, recording, and cleaning up of the audio might take longer than an hour, the fee is calculated based on the finished hour. This setup is particularly beneficial as it gives you a clear understanding of the overall cost.

Our target should be books around 30,000 words. This is because approximately 10,000 words translate into an hour of narration. Hence, 30,000 words would result in about three hours of content — the sweet spot we aim for. For a three-hour audiobook, Audible rewards us with approximately a $7 royalty. If the audiobook falls short at two hours and fifty-nine minutes, the royalty drops to about $3. However, an audiobook lasting between five and ten hours will fetch about $10. So, in layman's terms, the 3-5 hour range yields the highest payment for the fewest words. It's crucial to note that Audible sets the prices, not us, and these are determined by the length of the audiobook. Below are more details on the royalty structure:

Audiobook Length	Retail Price	Net Sales $
< 1hr	3.95	2.05
1-3 hrs	6.95	3.61
3-5 hrs	14.95	7.77
5-10 hrs	19.95	10.37
10-20 hrs	24.95	12.97
20 hrs +	29.95	15.57

If your 30,000-word audiobook doesn't stretch to the three-hour mark, chances are the narrator read too quickly. It typically takes about 27,000 words spoken at a normal pace to hit the three-hour mark, so 30,000 words should more than suffice. Be sure to communicate your desired length with the narrator ahead of time to avoid any last-minute surprises.

My Reflections

When you're starting out on your author journey, diving straight into the world of audiobooks may not be necessary. Instead, I suggest you center your efforts on crafting a few quality books first. Get familiar with the process, understand the nuances, and gather some writing experience under your belt before you explore the realm of audiobooks. Once your books start generating a monthly income of at least $500, that's a good time to consider branching out into audiobooks. This approach also has a financial advantage. The income generated from your books can be funneled into covering the narration cost for your audiobook, which for a 30,000-word book, will typically start around $150.

17

PRICING YOUR BOOKS

Pricing your books is not just about making money but also about attracting customers to purchase your books. Finding the right balance between a fair price and broad customer appeal is crucial.

Pricing Low-Content Books

Low-content books, such as journals, planners, coloring books, and activity books are usually sold anywhere between $3.99 to $9.99. The sweet spot is $6.99 giving you a $2 profit per book. It's usually very difficult to sell a book higher than this as there is so much competition of high quality books at a lower price. Another reason why you should generally stay away from these types of books.

Pricing Fiction Books

If you're venturing into the world of fiction, understanding pricing in this genre is crucial. Whether you're going the traditional publishing route or self-publishing on Amazon, fiction book prices generally lean towards the lower side, and they tend to decrease over time. Even a bestselling author's hardcover might start at $19.99, but it quickly drops to $9.99 or even $6.99 for the paperback edition. EBooks, on the other hand, can sell for as low as a dollar or two. So, if you're a self-published author, it's not feasible to price your first fiction book at $20 or even $10. Instead, focus on building an audience and consider enrolling in Kindle Select to earn a portion of Kindle Unlimited membership fees. **At the beginning, your aim is to gain visibility, rankings, and positive reviews, with significant profits coming later.**

But why are fiction books priced so low? Well, the fiction genre boasts a wide readership, and self-published authors continuously release new books, often with shorter word counts. While traditionally published novels average around 80,000 words or more, self-published books can be as short as 30,000 words. This allows avid readers, who devour multiple books each week, to have a greater selection to choose from.

Pricing Non-Fiction Books

Setting the right price for non-fiction books requires a different strategy. Non-fiction works often offer valuable information, expertise, or unique perspectives to readers. Therefore, pricing should reflect the book's value and the perceived benefit it provides. Generally, non-fiction books tend to have higher price points compared to fiction. The exact range varies depending on factors such as the subject matter, depth of research, and the author's credentials. Readers are willing to pay more for specialized knowledge, well-researched content, and practical guidance.

When determining the price for your non-fiction book, it's essential to consider your target audience, the competitive landscape, and the unique selling points of your work. Conduct market research, analyze similar titles, and gauge what readers are willing to pay for the specific subject matter you cover.

Personally, I price my non-fiction books in the range of $12.99 to $19.99, taking into account the competitors and their pricing. If you have more reviews than your competitors, you can justify a higher price point. However, if there is significant competition with lower prices, it's advisable to stay within that ballpark. A safe approach to testing pricing is to start with a lower price and gradually increase it by a dollar every two weeks. Monitor your sales during this period. If they remain stable, you can continue raising the price until you observe a drop in sales.

Hardcovers

When it comes to pricing hardcovers, I usually set the price $10 higher than the paperback edition. There are three reasons behind this approach.

Firstly, it costs more to produce hardcovers and, in order to receive a comparable royalty, the price needs to be higher.

Secondly, it involves a concept called price anchoring. Price anchoring is a psychological technique that influences how people perceive prices. To illustrate, imagine looking at a restaurant menu where high-priced steaks are listed at $100. Then you come across a burger priced at $40. Initially, the $40 burger appears more affordable when compared to the $100 steaks. This is because the higher-priced steaks act as an anchor, making the burger seem like a better value in comparison. By utilizing price anchoring, the restaurant strategically influences customers to view the $40 burger as a better value, increasing the likelihood of them choosing it over other options.

By setting a higher price for hardcovers, it creates a price anchor that influences readers' perception of the paperback's price. The paperback then appears relatively less expensive and offers better value.

The third reason is that some readers prefer hardcovers and are willing to pay the higher price. By pricing hardcovers at $24.99 or $29.99, for example, authors can generate a nice royalty of $10 or more per book sold.

In summary, pricing hardcovers higher than paperbacks serves multiple purposes: accounting for production costs, utilizing price anchoring to enhance the perceived value of the paperback, and attracting readers who prefer hardcovers, thereby increasing royalty earnings.

18

MARKETING & SOCIAL MEDIA

Throughout my journey as an author, I've experimented with various marketing methods. With my prior experience with the Instagram platform, I decided to start here. I successfully grew an account to over 200,000 followers for one of my brands, but I realized that the return on investment wasn't worth it. The time and effort spent on Instagram could have been better utilized in creating more books. The stress and hassle of daily posting and content creation outweighed the sales generated.

I also dabbled in Facebook ads, but they proved to be expensive and yielded low conversion rates. The multi-step process of grabbing users' attention, getting them to read the ad, click on it, visit the product page on Amazon, add to cart, and ultimately make a purchase proved challenging.

Based on my experiences, social media marketing didn't yield significant results. While others may excel in this area or choose to hire marketing agencies, it requires valuable time, money, and mental bandwidth. In my opinion, it's not the most effective approach.

Returning to the 80/20 rule, it's important to focus on strategies that truly work and generate revenue. Does starting an Instagram account directly bring in money? Does creating a Facebook group or accumulating likes translate into profits? Does reposting tweets or pinning pins on Pinterest result in financial gains? The answer is no.

However, there is one method I've found to be a worthwhile time investment, especially if you plan to create multiple books under the same pen name or brand: collecting emails. You can include a QR code at the back of your book, inviting readers to sign up for additional bonus material. By building an email list, you can reach out to these individuals when you release another book. They are more likely to purchase again since they've already bought from you. Additionally, you can email them and kindly request reviews for your book, enhancing its visibility.

Setting up an email collection system is a one-time effort that runs in the background. Once your book is live on Amazon and generating sales, you will automatically start receiving emails to your list.

The email software I use is called Convertkit. At the time of this writing you can sign up for free and collect 1,000 emails before you have to begin paying. They have a bunch of great tutorials on their site on how to set up a simple email opt in (this is where you collect their email).

In return, you have to offer the customer a 'freebie.' This can also be called a lead magnet, which is a valuable incentive or resource offered to potential subscribers or lead. It serves as a way to attract and engage your target audience.

Lead magnets are designed to address a specific problem or provide a solution, catering to the interests and needs of your target audience. Here are some examples of lead magnets for different niches:

· · ·

E-commerce

▪ Exclusive discounts or coupons: Offer a special discount code or a percentage off their first purchase in exchange for their email address.

▪ Free shipping guide: Provide a downloadable guide on how to get free shipping on online purchases.

Health and Fitness

▪ Meal plan or recipe eBook: Offer a free eBook with healthy recipes or a meal plan guide.

▪ Workout video or fitness guide: Provide access to a video workout session or a comprehensive fitness guide.

Personal Development

▪ Goal-setting worksheet: Offer a downloadable worksheet to help individuals set and achieve their goals.

▪ Productivity toolkit: Provide a toolkit with productivity resources, such as templates, checklists, and guides.

Finance

▪ Budgeting template: Offer a spreadsheet template or an app recommendation to help individuals manage their finances effectively.

▪ Investment guide: Provide an eBook or a series of videos on investment strategies and tips.

. . .

Marketing and Business

▪ Social media content calendar: Offer a pre-made content calendar to help businesses plan their social media posts.

▪ Marketing toolkit: Provide a collection of marketing templates, guides, and resources.

Travel

▪ Destination guide: Offer a downloadable guide with insider tips and recommendations for a popular travel destination.

▪ Packing checklist: Provide a checklist of essential items to pack for different types of trips.

Remember, the key to a successful lead magnet is to make it valuable, relevant, and aligned with the interests of your target audience. It should provide a quick win or a solution to a problem they are facing, while also showcasing your expertise and building trust.

19

AMAZON ADS FOR AUTHORS

When it comes to selling books, targeting customers who are already on Amazon, ready to make a purchase, makes the process much smoother. That's why I choose to advertise my books exclusively on Amazon using their own advertising platform.

It may seem counterintuitive to pay for ads on the same platform where your books are already published, however, the truth is that you're up against countless other books, and unless you have an instant best-seller, utilizing Amazon Advertising becomes crucial to gain visibility and drive sales for your paperbacks. According to Amazon's data, 30% of readers often browse Amazon specifically for books, and 65% actually discover new books while shopping on the platform. This means there's a receptive and eager market out there, and advertising provides a chance to reach customers who are actively exploring various book categories.

Different Advertising Methods

Amazon offers three distinct methods for advertising books. The first is Sponsored Products, which are cost-per-click (CPC) ads that promote individual product listings on Amazon. These ads prominently appear on the first page of search results and product pages. You can set your desired CPC bid and only pay when a customer clicks on your ad. By setting a daily budget, you can effectively control your costs.

The second option is Sponsored Brands, another CPC ad format that showcases your brand logo, a brief headline, and multiple products. These ads are positioned at the top and bottom of search results, making them ideal if you have several similar books, like a series. Similar to Sponsored Product Ads, you only pay when a customer clicks on your ad, and you have control over the per-click price and daily budget.

Lastly, there are Lockscreen Ads, which are exclusive to publishers in the United States. These ads appear on Amazon devices such as Kindle e-readers and Fire tablets, displaying your book prominently on the screen before users open their devices. However, it's worth noting that Lockscreen Ads can be more expensive and are typically utilized by successful authors with a substantial following.

For most self-published authors, the main focus is on Sponsored Product Ads and Sponsored Brand Ads, as they are easier to manage and learn. Personally, I've found success using only Sponsored Product Ads, which have proven to be profitable for me.

I would recommend starting there and, if you achieve positive results, you can venture out and try the Sponsored Brand Ads. I advise against utilizing Lockscreen Ads, as I believe they aren't as effective. As a Kindle owner myself, I rarely pay attention to the ads on my screen and have since turned them off so I can't even see them. It's unlikely that someone would see an ad, click on it, and then make a purchase of your book.

Getting Started With Ads

To embark on your Amazon Advertising journey, the initial step is creating an account at advertising.amazon.com. This process is simple and completely free. As you'll be investing in ads, you'll need to provide a payment method, such as a debit or credit card. Alternatively, you can set up a bank account for direct withdrawals. Once your account is active, you're ready to set up your first ad.

Inside the Amazon Advertising dashboard, a blue "Create campaign" button awaits, leading you to the campaign creation page. There, you'll encounter the options of Sponsored Products, Sponsored Brands, or Lockscreen Ads. Start with the default option, Sponsored Products, and continue by clicking the appropriate icon.

The first section you'll encounter is Ad Format, where you'll make a choice between a Custom text ad or a Standard ad. Custom text ads empower you to add personalized text, giving customers a glimpse of your book. On the other hand, Standard ads display your book cover, star rating, and price. For non-fiction books, both options work well, as the cover should effectively convey the book's content. However, Custom text ads can be particularly advantageous for fiction books facing substantial competition. Let's select the Standard ad for this example.

Moving forward, you'll reach the Products section, where you'll specify the book you wish to advertise. If applicable, you can choose both the Kindle and paperback versions. However, it's advisable to solely run ads for the paperback. This is because customers can see the price before clicking the ad, making them more likely to purchase at that price. Advertising a $2.99 eBook could result in unprofitable campaigns, as you'll end up spending more than $2 in ad costs to acquire a customer, resulting in a $2 profit.

Next, you'll need to decide on Targeting: Automatic or Manual. For beginners, Automatic Targeting is a suitable choice. Amazon utilizes targeted keywords and products similar to your ads content, effectively matching your book with relevant options in the market. As you gain experience, Manual Targeting provides greater control, enabling you to select specific keywords or products for your ad to appear alongside. Opting for Automatic Targeting will lead you to selecting the default bid, which is recommended to start low and increase later if necessary. If you choose Manual Targeting, you'll proceed to select between Keyword targeting or Product targeting.

Keyword targeting allows you to handpick specific keywords and short phrases that customers commonly search for on Amazon. You have the flexibility to create your own list, use Amazon's suggested keywords, or employ a combination of both. On the other hand, Product targeting permits you to directly target specific products, categories, or brands.

In our example of creating a Keyword Targeting ad for a Ketogenic cookbook, selecting the book prompts Amazon to generate a list of related keywords based on customers' active searches. Remember that customers often use short phrases when searching. Amazon's auto-fill suggestions provide valuable insights into popular keywords. These suggestions could include "ketogenic diet recipes," "low-carb cooking," and "healthy fat recipes." Even if some keywords may initially seem unrelated to your book, they indicate active purchasing behavior, making them effective targets.

Returning to the Amazon Advertising page, you have options to use Amazon's suggested keywords, enter your own list, or upload a file containing a keyword list. For simplicity, let's focus on utilizing the suggested keywords or entering your own list.

Before selecting keywords, it's crucial to decide on your bidding price. Next to Bid, you'll notice a bar displaying Suggested bid. Clicking on it reveals a drop-down menu with three choices: Suggested bid, Custom bid, and Default bid. Initially, I made the mistake of relying on the Suggested bids, which often exceeded the necessary amounts for effective ads. Using these bids can quickly deplete your advertising budget. Instead, I recommend selecting Custom bid, allowing you to set the same rate for each keyword. Starting with a very low bid is recommended. Amazon's suggested bids generally fall within the range of 50 cents to $1, sometimes even higher. Instead, enter a low Custom bid of 30 cents to commence. Opting for an odd number like 21 cents can enhance competitiveness, as most advertisers prefer even numbers.

Once you've set your bid rate, it's time to choose your keywords. Amazon classifies keywords into three types: Broad, Phrase, and Exact.

Broad: Your keywords will be matched with search terms that correspond to your keywords and related keywords, including synonyms, misspellings, and variations. For example, selecting "Ketogenic Cookbook" as a Broad keyword could display your ad alongside books that appear in searches for terms like "Ketogeniccookbook" (misspelled), "Ketogenic Cookbooks" or "Keto cookbook."

Phrase: Your keywords will be matched with search terms that include the specific keywords in any order. For instance, the keyword "Ketogenic Cookbook" could place your ad next to books that appear in searches using phrases like "Vegan Ketogenic Cookbook" or "Ketogenic Cookbook for beginners."

Exact: Your keywords will only be matched with those that precisely match them. For example, selecting the keyword "Ketogenic Cookbook" as Exact would show your ad to users who searched using "Ketogenic Cookbook" as the sole search term.

When starting out, it's acceptable to select all three options. Amazon generally pre-selects them by default. Over time, you'll discover which type works best for you. Some advertisers stick to a single type, while others employ two or all three. You can also allow Amazon to show you all three and manually choose your preferred options. Amazon will provide a comprehensive list of suggested keywords. Although you can click "Add all" to select all of them, it's recommended to review the options, as irrelevant keywords might be included. Manually selecting the keywords you want to use and skipping the irrelevant ones is a prudent approach.

After choosing your keywords, the subsequent section is Negative keyword targeting, an optional but helpful feature. It enables you to exclude search terms that Amazon might use to target your ad but are irrelevant to your book. For example, if you've written a book on *Personal finance for teenagers*, you wouldn't want your ad shown to people searching for "personal finance for adults." By entering negative keywords, you prevent Amazon from wasting impressions and clicks on customers searching for a different book genre. Maintaining a document with lists of negative keywords for each of your books is useful. When setting up a new ad campaign, you can manually enter negative keywords by typing them or copying them from a file. Remember to add negative keywords as both Negative exact and Negative phrase to ensure their effective exclusion.

. . .

Campaigns

The next section to explore is Campaign, where you'll have the opportunity to choose your Campaign bidding strategy. Amazon presents three options for your consideration:

Dynamic bids - down only: With this strategy, Amazon will dynamically lower your bids in real-time when the likelihood of your ad converting to a sale decreases.

Dynamic bids - up and down: Opting for this strategy allows Amazon to dynamically raise your bids by up to 100% when the chances of your ad leading to a sale increase, while also lowering bids when the likelihood decreases.

Fixed bids: This strategy maintains your exact bid and any manual adjustments you've made, without changing your bids based on the likelihood of a sale.

To exercise control over costs, I personally choose Dynamic bids - down only. By granting Amazon the ability to only lower your bid or adhere to the bid price you set, you can avoid excessive spending on ads.

Moving on to the Settings section, you'll commence by selecting a Campaign name. This can be the title of your book or a descriptive name that helps distinguish each ad if you plan to run multiple ads for the same book. Duplicate names for ads are not permitted in the system. As for my own naming convention, I usually follow the format of "Book name - manual/PA (product ad)/auto" e.g.

1. Ketogenic (manual)

2. Ketogenic (PA)

3. Ketogenic (auto)

In the Start and End dates section, by default, the date will be set to the day you create the ad. It's generally advisable to leave the end date as "No end date." If you need to pause or stop the ad, it's best to turn it off directly from the main dashboard.

The Marketplace section operates automatically, selecting the marketplace based on your advertising country. For instance, if your account is established in the United States, the United States marketplace will already be pre-selected. It's worth noting that initially, it's recommended to focus on the US market, as it is the largest one. Once you have a book that gains significant traction and achieves substantial monthly earnings ($500+), you can then consider expanding your advertising efforts to other markets.

Next, it's essential to determine your daily budget. Starting with a conservative budget of $5 is recommended. If your ad demonstrates success, you can later increase your ad spending accordingly.

Once you've finalized the settings, you have the choice to save your ad as a draft or proceed by clicking the blue "Launch campaign" button if you're ready for it to go live. Rest assured that you can edit or end your ads at any time, so there's no need to worry if you made a mistake along the way.

20

CONCLUSION

The world of self-publishing is like a treasure trove for budding authors. It's a place where you can live out your publishing dreams without the red tape that comes with traditional publishing houses. Plus, you get to call the shots on your creative journey and pocket a bigger chunk of the earnings.

But remember, self-publishing isn't just about pouring out your thoughts on paper. It involves some serious tasks like getting your file formatting right, creating a cover that turns heads, and managing a promo game that hits the bullseye. It requires your time and effort, no two ways about it. But hey, with the handy advice in this book, you'll be navigating your way to financial success in the self-publishing world like a pro.

Reflecting on my journey, I noticed that out of my first ten books, only one turned out to be successful (generating over $1,000 per month). Keep this nugget of wisdom tucked away. Your breakthrough may not come until you've written a few books, and that's perfectly alright. The only true failure is giving up. Persist in your efforts and your chances of success will undoubtedly escalate. Remember, this book is here to guide you, helping you bypass the pitfalls I encountered. This should fast-track your path to not just success, but also accelerated monetary gains!

Engage with the vibrant self-publishing community thriving on various online platforms like Facebook groups, YouTube channels, and social media communities. Discover the invaluable wisdom shared by accomplished authors already earning substantial income through self-published books. Staying informed about the ever-evolving landscape is pivotal to avoid being left behind. To stay abreast of the latest information, tips, tricks, and hacks in publishing, I encourage you to join my email list by signing up by clicking (if you're on a Kindle) or scanning the QR code below:

In the self-publishing world, success lies in the mantra of "write, publish, repeat." The more books you offer for sale, the greater your chances of financial prosperity and building a thriving author career. Each publication contributes to your growth as a writer, refining your cover designs and honing your overall publishing process. Through sharing the invaluable lessons I've learned, my intention is to smooth your path to your self-publishing success.

. . .

To recap, remember the essential elements of a successful book:

1. Researching to find a profitable keyword.

2. Creating an outline.

3. Writing out the book or getting a ghost writer to write it.

4. Editing your book or getting an editor to edit it.

5. Formatting your book or getting a formatter to format it.

6. Creating your cover or getting a designer to design it.

7. Uploading your eBook, paperback, and hardcover to KDP.

8. Creating ads for your book.

Now, the moment has arrived for you to embark on your writing journey and seize the opportunity to generate income through self-publishing your books with Amazon KDP!

<h1 style="text-align:center">All Links</h1>

KDP account creation

kdp.amazon.com/signin

Keyword research software

https://authorpreneuracademy--leadsclick.thrivecart.com/kdspy-v5/

BSR viewer

https://chrome.google.com/webstore/detail/ds-amazon-quick-view/jkompbllimaoekaogchhkmkdogpkhojg

Pen name generator

https://blog.reedsy.com/pen-name-generator/

Paperback cover generator

https://kdp.amazon.com/en_US/cover-calculator

Design software

www.canva.com

Email marketing software

https://app.convertkit.com/users/signup?plan=free-limited&lmref=Lz6sJQ

Amazon advertising

http://advertising.amazon.com

100 Covers

https://100covers.com/

Upwork

https://www.upwork.com/

Fiverr

https://www.fiverr.com/

If you want all the links on one neatly organized clickable PDF, scan the QR code, enter your email and I'll send it to you!

Thank you!

If the insights you've gained from this book have been valuable to you, they could be equally beneficial for others. Extend a helping hand today by taking 30 seconds to leave a review. Your thoughts might be the very guidance someone else needs on their self-publishing path. Thank you for sharing this journey with me!

Simply scan the QR code to be directed to the Amazon page, where you can effortlessly leave your valuable review.

Printed in Great Britain
by Amazon

41382429R00069